ILLUSTRATED
HISTORY
OF THE WORLD

An encyclopaedia of events from
pre-historic times up to the present day

Translated from the French edition by
Rosemary Arundale and Tony Mertz

CLIVEDEN PRESS

FOREWORD

It has been said that knowledge is but recorded experience and a product of history. This clearly expresses the motives that guided us in the writing of this book. Our greatest concern has been to give young readers and their families a book that is both instructive and interesting, with easy reference.

But in such a vast panorama of history it becomes a question of condensing the material so that events and people are clearly placed in context of the times and so that similar events happening in different parts of the world may be compared and related. Even if this material is sometimes schematic, the reader will get a clear and complete view of the particular period in history, and will be able to draw conclusions which, in the final analysis, are the lessons to be learned from history.

What happened in Asia while the Seven Years' War was raging in Europe? Had the Arabs left Spain when Christopher Colombus was discovering America? Was Michelangelo alive during the reign of Charles V? This book proposes to answer these questions, and others, about which memory is often at fault.

The illustrations accompanying the text help the reader more vividly to picture the people and the events. Moreover, following each double-page of text are two pages of paintings and engravings relating to the period. This combination of text and pictures gives the reader a richer and more complete view of history.

The table of contents, which appears at the end of the book, permits rapid reference to the desired period.

THE EDITORS

Giant dinosaurs and plesiosauri.

1. Algae. 2. Sponges.
3. Platyhelminths.
4. Radiolarians.

1. Armour-plated fish.
2. Crinoids. 3. Mollusca.
4. Trilobites.

Primitive amphibian.

Astronomers and physicists estimate that five thousand million years have elapsed since the elements combined to create the physical world in which we live today. It is imagined that at first there was shapeless matter which formed itself into atoms provided with electronic satellites; then a chain reaction developed which produced the light and the millions of galaxies in the universe. Some two thousand million years later, a particle of cosmic matter, from the sun or a star, was shot into space following an atomic explosion.

Little by little, this particle had to find its orbit around the sun and its rotation on its own axis. After another thousand million years the earth's crust was formed, water began to flow on the surface and sediments were deposited. It was in these waters that life was first born.

There is not very much known of the period from the formation of primitive cells to the appearance of very simple living beings such as protozoa and algae. Four hundred million years ago the first vertebrae—fish—appeared. The algae gradually pushed out into the humid shores of the oceans and scorpions and centipedes began to breathe the air.

Vegetation slowly spread across the earth, which, in three hundred million years would be covered over with immense forests of giant ferns and conifers. Eventually these forests, swallowed by upheavals of the earth, would be formed into coal seams.

The first insects lived in the swamps and oceans, which abounded with dragonflies. Then came the first amphibians, the frogs. Reptiles, in their turn, came to conquer the earth.

The primary or Palaeozoic era had finished and the Mesozoic era was beginning. After 150 million years, the ferns disappeared and other plants began to bear flowers. This was the age of the saurians, the giant animals with tiny heads, such as dinosaurs, which stood on their hind legs, rather like kangaroos, gaining balance from their tails.

The air now became populated, just as had the land and sea before it. Certain creatures were endowed with membranes which made them into flying reptiles. The first known bird, the archaeopteryx, was a like species but it was provided with wings and feathers.

Finally the first mammals appeared. They were small hairy quadrupeds, like large rats, which fed their young with their own milk and lived in families and groups.

These factors helped them to survive the cataclysm which swallowed up

Scene from the beginning
of the Ice Age

Primitive insect

the saurians into the ice at the end of the Mesozoic era. It also helped them to breed in the third or Cenozoic era.

Going back seventy million years ago, we witness the first appearance of animals which we know today: elephants, rhinoceruses, antelopes, stags, zebras, tigers, wolves, foxes, pigs and hedgehogs.

Volcanic eruptions gave birth to great ranges of mountains, the Himalayas, Alps, Caucasus and Rocky Mountains. The sub-tropical forests were buried and the seas pushed back.

Anthropoids then appeared, the gibbon to begin with, and then his later companions: the orang-utan, gorilla and chimpanzee. They had a more developed brain than other animals and stood on their hind legs.

Man's earliest ancestor, Australopithecus, stood upright about five feet in height and was essentially human in form. Traces of these ancestors of man have been found in southern Africa dating back 600,000, or perhaps even a million years.

Their successors, Pithecanthropus and Sinanthropus (600000—180000), began to think for themselves. They invented the first tools—rough flints— and used fire for domestic purposes. Fire was their only source of power at this time when the earth was undergoing successive periods of glaciation.

Stone spearhead

Neanderthal man (180000—50000) had a fixed home—his cave. He dressed in animal skins, perfected his tools by adding handles, and buried his dead with ceremony, proving that there was already some religious feeling.

Sixty thousand years ago, groups of men moved across Asia, Africa and Europe. They settled down and formed tribes, the first form of a fixed social structure.

Cro-Magnon (Homo Sapiens), the species of man existing at the end of the Paleolithic era of the Stone Age, became very capable of organising their lives. The caves where they still lived, before moving to mud houses, were lit with lamps made of animal fat. They made needles of bone and ivory, and jewellery from shells, amber and coral.

Instead of the coarse hatchets of their predecessors, they had fine, pointed weapons and bows and arrows. The scenes painted on the walls of the caves at Lascaux, Altamira and the Sahara, depicting bison, mammoths, bears and leaping reindeer are marvellous evidence of the life of this time, a life dedicated to the chase.

Cave painter

A Danish Dolmen. Dolmens, formed from huge uncut boulders, are probably ancient tombs.

Detail from a cave painting discovered in the Sahara. Animals were the dominant theme in the art of prehistoric man.

Primitive bronze scissors.

A bone chisel, reproduced to exact size.

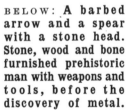

BELOW: A barbed arrow and a spear with a stone head. Stone, wood and bone furnished prehistoric man with weapons and tools, before the discovery of metal.

OPPOSITE: Imprints left in rock by an ancient species of leaf. Prints and tracks such as these are classed as fossils as well as actual remains.

Primitive agriculture

The Temple of Babylon

Ancient Egyptian oven

Sumerian hieroglyphics

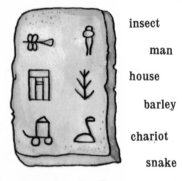

insect

man

house

barley

chariot

snake

Sumerian cuneiform
writing

So, probably stemming from magic, the first expressions of a religious feeling, Art was born.

With the passing of the civilisation of the hunters, evolution became very rapid. It is only ten thousand years since man first began to tame animals, using some of them to pull his carts. Employing the tools that he now sharpened with a grindstone, he worked the earth, cultivating and producing large quantities of corn and wheat.

He began to fashion clay, to weave wool. Soon he thought of exchanging the things he made and grew for other things he needed. Commerce was thus born in the Neolithic Era, or New Stone Age, 7000—4000 BC.

Paleolithic man was a hunter and gatherer of wild foods, with a limited inventory of tools; but Neolithic man dominated his environment. Agriculture, animal domestication, pottery making and house building all appeared first in the Neolithic Age.

Man fully developed the discovery of metal and the knowledge of working with metals. At first copper was used; then, through melting and blending with tin, bronze was discovered. Iron was not generally used until a later period, as it was considered at first to be even more precious than gold and silver.

A community life was organised. Only a disciplined people could have erected such structures as those of Carnac and Stonehenge and the villages on stilts in Switzerland. Soon, towns would be born, states and empires. This was the beginning of history.

The first great civilisations began in the fertile valleys of large rivers—the Euphrates and Tigris, the Nile, the Indus and the Yellow River.

Remains of early cities built between 5000 and 4000 BC have been found in the Indus valley. We know that, about 2500 BC, the cities of Mohenjo-Daro and Harappa in this area were built in a chequered pattern, with wide roads, brick houses of several stories, running water and main-drainage.

There were no temples, but there was an organised administrative life and active commercial trade, proved by the thousands of letters recovered from the ruins. These letters were engraved with inscriptions which have, as yet, not been translated. Mesopotamia, where Sumerians, Semites and Indo-Europeans were to succeed each other for three thousand years, underwent several different civilisations.

Probably coming from the Armenian plateaux about 3000 BC, the Sumerians settled in the delta of the Tigris and Euphrates rivers. They built dykes and

8

Building the Egyptian pyramids

Egyptian hieroglyphics

dams and founded the city of Ur on the Persian Gulf. Before silver came into use as money, they used their rich harvests of corn as commercial currency. Their government was a theocracy, the kings representing the gods, and the temple, with its vast terraces, occupied the most important position in their towns.

One of their great contributions to civilisation was handwriting, which at first took the form of drawings called hieroglyphics, then developed into symbolical signs.

As it was impressed on moist clay, with the aid of a wedge shape, this type of writing was known as 'cunéiforme'.

Egyptian gods

Another innovation was administrative organisation. Scribes kept the public accounts, saw that all taxes were paid and decided whom to employ.

Now we see the appearance of the Semites, who for a long time had been mixing with the Sumerians. One of them, King Sargon I, unified Mesopotamia and built his capital at Akkad. This kingdom, which stretched from Elam in the East as far as the Mediterranean in the West, far from destroyed the Sumerian civilisation but helped to spread it. The Empire collapsed as a result of the invasions of the hill-folk, the Guti, and a century of anarchy followed.

Order was reintroduced under the kings of Ur and Babylon.

During this time another valley, that of the Nile, had produced one of the most lasting empires the world has yet seen.

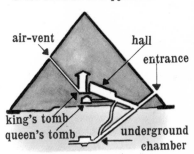

Cross-section of a pyramid

air-vent — hall — entrance — king's tomb — queen's tomb — underground chamber

Five thousand years ago, African tribes came from Abyssinia and settled in the North of Egypt. They lived with others from Mesopotamia and Arabia. From this mixture was born a race whose proud features we see engraved on the walls of Egyptian tombs.

These people grouped together in villages and each man had his own talisman—a falcon, a jackal or a gazelle. They were governed by a kind of council of ancients. This was the foreshadowing of the great Egyptian Empire.

Two distinct kingdoms were formed—that of the North, whose god was Seth, and the kingdom of the South, who worshipped Horus. The two were united about 3000 BC by King Menes, who was noted for the double-wreathed head-dress he wore, a symbol of the two Egypts united. This remained as the royal insignia of the Pharaohs.

The life of these agricultural people was centred around one annual event—the flooding of the Nile. They studied the stars so that they could foresee the ebb and flow of the river, and in this way astronomy was developed.

Egyptian scribe

OPPOSITE, RIGHT: The base of a pyramid at Gizeh near Cairo. Each block of stone weighs about 2 tons. Without the use of cranes, motors or even wheels, the early Egyptians raised these enormous masses by an ingenious system of inclined planes.

LEFT: Mesopotamian statue in copper from about 3,000 BC.

Sculpture from the palace of Khorsabad in Iraq

The ruins of Babylon

Sumerian cuneiform inscription on a tablet of clay. These tablets were mainly used by merchants.

Bullfighting scene in a Cretan palace

**Cultivating the fields.
In the background is a tomb.**

Vase of baked clay

House on stilts

Phoenician alphabet

𐤀 𐤄 𐤋 𐤌 𐤎

A E L M S

At a very early period they established a calendar of 365 days. The need to continually measure and remeasure their lands contributed to the development of geometry. Their religious development reveals the pastoral and agricultural origins of these people. Their gods had the bodies of humans but with animals' heads, such as the jackal-headed Anubis, and Hathor, the cow. Other gods favoured the harvest—Tefnut, goddess of moisture, and Osiris, goddess of vegetation. Besides their deities, the Egyptians worshipped beasts, reptiles and even vegetables, probably as symbols. They believed in the transmigration of souls and in the existence of a future state in which mankind would be rewarded or punished according to its actions while on earth.

Hieroglyphic writing appeared about 3000 years ago. It was first deciphered by Champollion at the beginning of the nineteenth century after Napoleon Bonaparte's Egyptian campaign.

Hieroglyphics is a form of writing in pictures. It could be written in ink on papyrus or just as well engraved on stone.

The Ancient Egyptian Empire, of which Memphis was the capital, lasted nearly 600 years (2778—2263 BC). It began with a period of great prosperity during which trade with Central Africa and the Middle East became more and more frequent. The Pharaohs, who were the absolute monarchs and venerated as gods, were trustees of all the lands. They governed by the intermediary of a strongly centralised administration—scribes, district chiefs and technicians who controlled the masses.

They organised the harvests and stored the grain, deducted taxes and maintained the dykes and waterworks.

The priests were all under the orders of the Pharaohs. The reverence for the dead, founded on their belief in a second life, was an important factor in their lives and explains their colossal tombs. The age of the great pyramid builders lasted until about 2500 BC. King Djoser ordered the building of a pyramid 196 feet tall in 2400 BC, and between the years 2400 and 2300 BC pyramids were built reaching heights of almost 460 feet.

From the entrance, which always faced the North, the galleries of the pyramids led to the burial chamber of the Pharaoh, who was mummified in a magnificent sarcophagus. He was surrounded by statues, objects from his everyday life and his subjects' offerings.

The age of the Pharaohs ended as they gradually lost their official capacity of sacred trustee of Egyptian soil, and surrendered their lands to their dignitaries. Struggles with the chiefs of townships gave rise to misery and suffering.

The Hebrews crossing the Sinai desert

Scribes, peasants and merchants all revolted. Finally, the Ancient Egyptian Empire drew to a close with the kidnapping of the Pharaoh Pepi II.

The European countries were then barely out of the Stone Age. But centres of rural civilisation were beginning to form, distinguished by the dwellings on stilts, the cromlechs and tumuli, or ancient sepulchral mounds which have since been excavated.

Now we are approaching the world as it was some 2000 years before our own time. About this period, bands of warriors came from Central Asia, overrunning the Indus valley and destroying the cities of Harappa and Mohenjo-Daro. It was the first of the Indo-European invasions which, during the following thousand years, totally changed the structure of the oriental empires and of the Mediterranean world.

History began in the Mediterranean lands with the Cretans. A very advanced civilisation had flourished very early on the small island of Crete. Working in bronze, gold and silver and producing wines and oils, the Cretans sold their products all over the East. They exported their goods in their fast ships, propelled both by oars and sails, and the influence of their civilisation spread to the shores of Greece, Italy and Spain.

The Cretans built sumptuous palaces at Phaistos and Knossos which the Greeks called labyrinths, after the *labrys*, the double-headed hatchet which was the symbol of the king Minos. This is the king whose memory is linked with the legend of the Minotaur.

The walls of the Cretan palaces, and also the pottery work, were patterned with exquisite frescoes of ladies in elegant low-necked crinoline gowns. The scenes of games, feasts and dances depicted on their vases reveal a court life where luxury and pleasure assumed a high importance.

Bulls were sacred animals. Acrobats would sport with them, making the bulls toss them in the air so that they might somersault and land on their feet behind the animals.

In Mesopotamia, in reaction against the Guti barbarians, the kingdom of Ur had been constituted and there had ensued a century of peace in a unified country. But the struggle once again resumed between the different cities, and the capital, Ur, was razed and settled into the sand.

The Assyrians founded Assur near the Tigris and spread towards the North. In the East, the land of Elam formed itself into a kingdom with Susa as its capital. Between these two states, King Hammurabi once again unified Mesopotamia.

In Babylon, his capital, he developed a combination of the civilisations of

Neolithic bronze hatchet

Hammurabi

First Chinese characters:

𝍉	li	Standing upright
═	schang	above
─	hia	below
⚡	sche	archery
⚱	yu	wine

Rameses II

Rural scenes. Numerous tomb paintings describe for us the life of the Egyptian peasants. BELOW: A funeral barge, on which the dead man, accompanied by his relations, journeys along the Nile to the eternal resting place. The Egyptians believed in a second life, similar to the life on earth, and dependant on the preservation of the corpse. This belief led to the embalming of the bodies. Everyday objects were placed with the dead in the tombs, as well as statues of the slaves that had served them. For us this is a precious source of information on the ways and customs of Ancient Egypt.

The golden sarcophagus of Tutankhamen of the XVIIIth dynasty.

RIGHT: Fresco in the palace at Knossos, Crete. This palace was identified by the Greeks as the seat of the legendary King Minos.

BELOW: Ivory and gold statue of the snake goddess, reflecting the tasteful elegance of Cretan women.

BOTTOM: Ruins of the palace at Knossos. The pipelines in this vast labyrinth of buildings, covering an area of more than seven acres, carried running water.

Olympic Games

Phoenician ship

Greek writing

ΑΛΛΟΥΔΕΝΗΔΙΟΝ
ΕΜΟΙΓΕΕΕΙΜΗΤΥΓ
ΧΑΝΕΙΑΛΗΘΗΘΣΟΝ
ϹΡΡΑΣΟΝΔΕΜΟΙΤΙΣ
ΗΩΦΕΛΙΑΤΟΙΣΘΕ
ΟΙΣΤΥΓΧΑΝΕΙΟΥΣΑ

Egyptian potter

Romulus and Remus,
suckled by the She-Wolf

Akkad and Sumeria. *The Code of Hammurabi* (1730 BC) is the first known collection of laws. Under these rules men were divided into three classes: slaves, paupers and free men. These latter, amongst them the lords of the land, were responsible for the irrigation of their lands.

The code made rules for the most modern forms of commerce—fixing tariffs and salaries, organising the caravan communities and appointing the rates of loans. Tribunals were elected and punishments given according to the law of retaliation, the principle of 'an eye for an eye and a tooth for a tooth.'

In Egypt, after two centuries of disorder which followed the fall of the Ancient Empire, the kings of Thebes reunified the country. The Pharaohs of the Middle Kingdom organised a true socialist state. This prosperous period was clearly marked by the growth of trade with Somalia, Crete and Babylon.

The Middle Kingdom (2133—1680 BC) fell under the attacks of the invading Hyskos—Indo-European tribes who settled there for more than 100 years between 1670 and 1570 BC.

Egypt was reborn with the New Kingdom (1570—1085 BC) which was a military rule formed to fight against the disorder which had arisen in neighbouring Mesopotamia. The nomads of the mountains and plains were driven out: the Aryans to India, the Hittites to the North-West of Asia Minor and the Kassites to Babylon. The Pharaohs of Thebes consolidated their forces to take over Nubia, Syria and to push up to the Upper Euphrates.

All the lands of Mesopotamia were a tribute to the progress and civilisation of Egypt. The peak of the New Kingdom Era is marked by great buildings, like the temples of Amon Re at Karnak and Luxor.

In the XIVth century BC the Pharaoh Amenophis attempted to establish the worship of a single god, Aton. But this innovation was not maintained by his successors, and Tutankhamon re-established the traditional gods.

At the beginning of the XIIIth century BC, under Rameses II, Egypt had to relinquish Syria in her battles against the Hittites. It was at this time that the rock temple at Abu Simbel was built.

In the XIIth century BC, Rameses III repulsed the attacks of the 'people of the sea' for a time but, after his death, Egypt declined rapidly.

In the wave of Indo-European invasions, the Achaeans from the North had

Greek triremes with sail-hauling tackle

Spartan warrior

Serf

settled in Greece and created the kingdom of Mycenae. They had come under the influence of the Cretans, before laying waste the island that had educated them.

The Achaeans traded in the Aegean Sea, trying to win over the routes of gold and corn that passed by the Dardanelles. They were the conquerors of Troy, in Asia Minor, but were defeated by an invasion of the Dorians who brought with them the knowledge of iron and its uses.

In this period the domination of the sea belonged to the Phoenicians. These Semites had been settled for centuries on a narrow line of coast bordered by the mountains of the Lebanon. Since 1500 BC, the port of Byblos had afforded them great commercial activity which was bound to increase, after 1400, with Sidon and Tyr. In their large trading ships, which carried many types of goods—precious metals, transparent crystals and crimson-dyed cloths—the Phoenicians sailed the Mediterranean, even as far as the Atlantic Ocean, touching Morocco and Britain. They established warehouses all over the western Mediterranean coast.

The Phoenicians, in fact, opened to the world the door to the West.

Their other great contribution to the history of civilisation is their invention of the alphabet, later adopted by the Hebrews and then by the Greeks.

Amongst the Semitic people who came into Mesopotamia, Syria and Egypt, the Hebrews have a special place. We know from the Bible that these nomads left Egypt about 1250 BC through the Sinai desert, led by Moses, who wanted to lead the ' chosen people ' to the Promised Land.

They called themselves the chosen ones because they differed from the other people of the East on one major point—they believed in only one God.

On Mount Sinai, Moses received the Ten Commandments for his people from God. The Hebrews settled in the mountains in scattered tribes. Over the next 200 years they conquered the country of Canaan and continually struggled against the Philistines. Eventually, they settled down into one kingdom under King Saul.

Greek minstrel

King David unified the twelve tribes of Israel and took possession of Jerusalem, making it his religious and political capital.

Solomon gave great economic prosperity to Israel and a considerable cultural influence. On his death, in 978 BC, the kingdom was split into two states, Israel and Juda.

Israel fell in 732 BC to the Assyrians, and Juda only lasted until 587 BC, the

Solon

17

OPPOSITE, LEFT: **A model of Phoenician ship of 900 BC from the museum of Science and Technology, Milan. Skilful sailors and able technicians, the Phoenicians constructed their boats along similar lines to those used today. They began by making a solid casing which ended in a keel and covered it with a boarding made from squared planks caulked with Chaldean bitumen.**

RIGHT: **Phoenician votive statuettes found at Byblus (Lebanon).**

BOTTOM, LEFT: **Ruins of Olympia, the famous Greek town where, in 776 BC, the first Olympic games took place.**

Painting on a Greek vase representing a Homeric warrior, probably the fiery Achilles, hero of the Trojan War.

BELOW: **Only stumps of columns and a few wall remains are left of austere and glorious Sparta. Other, less ancient, ruins in the region date from the Roman era.**

Hebrews in captivity

Pythagoras' theorem

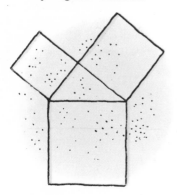

The tomb of Cyrus

Buddha

Confucius

date of the capture of Babylon. But, thanks to their prophets, the spiritual heritage of the Hebrews survived and later opened the door to Christianity.

In India, the Aryans carried on the system of castes, at the head of which were the Brahmins, originating from the god Brahma, the creator of nature. The Vedic Hymns, in the ancient Sanskrit language, are the sacred books of this religion.

In China, the peasants, grouped around local chiefs, cultivated the region of the Yellow River. The legendary Shang dynasty (1700—1100 BC) contributed to the birth of a brilliant civilisation. They began to weave silks and make ceramics. Their form of picture writing exists even today. About the first century BC, the prosperity of the Tsin Dynasty was considerable, and it was marked by an expansion in trade, both imports and exports.

Between the years 1000 and 800, the Greek world took its flight. The Achaeans from the cities of Asia Minor and the Dorians from European Greece took to the seas. They colonised the archipelago of the Aegean Sea, Crete and Rhodes. In about 750 they established themselves on the shores of the Black Sea, along the Hellespont and in Thrace. Using the Corinthian triremes—galleys with three ranks of oars, one above the other—they went to the west, to the towns of southern Italy, to Sicily, and to Marseilles. It was the epoch in which, according to legend, Romulus drew up the boundaries of Rome.

The Etruscans occupied the northern half of the Peninsula. In liaison with the Phoenician colony of Carthage they were to bring an end to the Greek expansion towards the west.

One of the main events in Greek development, the Trojan War, lives eternally in the *Iliad*. The *Odyssey*, while recounting the adventures of Ulysses, describes in reality the journey of the Greek merchants from colony to colony. These poems are attributed to Homer whose existence has sometimes been questioned by scholars who have held that the exploits of the Achaean heroes were probably handed down by bards who, like the minstrels in the Middle Ages, sang from house to house. According to modern opinion, however, Homer did live, between 1200 and 850 BC.

These poems of ancient Greece extol the culture of beauty which was to reveal itself in art. It had already expressed itself in the games, those glorious ceremonies, which were established at that time.

The Persian army crossing the
Hellespont

Greek teacher

Etruscan peasant

The Olympic Games were founded in 776 BC. These games were regarded also as a sacred trial, offered to the gods, in which the valour of men was proved. Unfortunate for the vanquished! The presidents of the Nemean games, created in 753, attended assemblies in mourning clothes.

In this harsh and fervent world everything was a test. The *Odyssey* shows us Ulysses and Diomedes leaving by night on a reconnaissance. Ulysses wears a head-dress decorated with the fangs of wild boars; Diomedes wears a lion skin. The objective is to surprise the spy Dolon, who is clothed in the hide of a grey wolf. If they fail, they are not worthy of being called 'men.'

Young men at that time were grouped into brotherhoods, which received the names of animals—amongst which the name 'wolf' was greatly favoured —as today we have the scouts and wolf cubs.

While Greek power increased, in the East the Assyrians had set out for the conquest of Mesopotamia. Their conquests included Babylon, Syria, Palestine and even part of Egypt, and behind them they left the pyramids decorated with the severed heads of their opponents in battle. The principal towns of their empire were Nineveh and Assur.

Their contribution to civilisation was of little importance; Assyria asserted itself above all as a martial power. Its downfall, marked in 612 by the destruction of Nineveh, was the result of an alliance between the Chaldeans, who had withdrawn to the heart of the Assyrian empire, and the Medes, an Indo-European nation who settled with the Persians on the plateau of Iran.

Nebuchadnezzar restored his power in Babylon, which was then that marvellous town where the palaces had hanging gardens and whose immense temple of Marduk was to be called, by the Hebrew captives, the Tower of Babel. For, in 587, Nebuchadnezzar took Jerusalem and led away the Hebrews into captivity.

In Greece, however, the cities became organised. The city was to be the sole type of state in the Greek world, each city having its own particular institutions.

In the Peloponnesus, the military state of Sparta was quick to establish itself. Under two powerless kings, the true masters were the five ephors, chief justices and executive officers, and the gerousia, a council of thirty men.

There were three classes: the citizens, trained from childhood by the most rigorous education and who served in the army; the perioeci, traders and artisans living on the outskirts of the city; and the wretched helots, serfs who

Roman tribune and senator

Pheidippides, messenger from
Marathon

Ten miles from Persepolis, in a place called Naksh-i-Rustam, in the rock which forms a high defensive wall, lie the tombs of the Achaemenid kings, the three Darius, Xerxes, and the three Artaxerxes.

LEFT: Lao-tse, Chinese philosopher, who doubtless lived in the seventh century BC. His teachings were propagated in China at almost the same time as those of Confucius, although the two teachings were directly opposed. While Confucius urged men towards moral and social virtues, Lao-tse advised abstention from all individual action, and surrender to the natural order of things, the principle which, to Lao, ruled the world. One particular interpretation of his doctrine gave birth to Taoism, a popular religion, rich in magical practice, far less noble and spiritual than was the original teaching.

BELOW: Ruins of Persepolis, founded in the sixth century BC by Darius I. The town was the capital of the Achaemenid kings until the destruction of the empire by Alexander the Great. It was situated on the edge of the route leading from Isfahan to Shiraz, in what is now Iran. The palaces, ornate with splendid carvings, were constructed in brick with stone doors.

A frieze in enamelled brick in Darius' palace at Susa (sixth century BC) illustrating an archer in the imperial guard.

Battle of Salamis

Fight between a Greek
and a Persian

Doric column

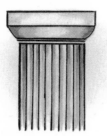

Ionian column

Corinthian column

worked the land of the citizens. This constitution was to remain unchanged. It was not the same in Athens, where democracy was soon to be adopted. After the kings, the power was assumed by the archons, magistrates chosen from the nobles. Before the revolt of the oppressed nation Draco proclaimed the first written laws.

In 594, Solon proclaimed political and economic reforms. He abolished debts—those citizens who had incurred debts had been subjected to slavery—and changed the monetary system. He repealed the harsh laws of Draco, except those relating to murder, which were retained.

In 560, Pisistratus seized control and again changed the order of things. He supported the poorer classes and, seizing the estates of his aristocratic opponents and distributing them amongst the needy, ended the strife between the rich and poor. Athens became peaceful and prosperous during his reign.

In 508, Cleisthenes established a democratic constitution. Under the jurisdiction of the city of Athens came the whole of Attica, which was divided into demes, or wards, which were grouped into ten tribes. Each tribe appointed an archon and five magistrates who sat at the boule, or council, at which all the important political decisions were taken, which were then approved by the ekklesia, or assembly of the people. The role of the aristocracy was thus greatly reduced.

Cleisthenes also introduced ostracism: the banishment of all citizens suspected of tyranny. One position of office, that of strategus, chief of the army and of the navy, was to become, owing to the wars, more important than that of archon. Slavery, that essential element of ancient economy, was, of course, in force in the Greek democracy.

Occupied by a mosaic of diverse nations, Italy was dominated by the Etruscans. Their cities, grouped together in a confederacy, were thriving. Their civilisation was very refined. Rome, in the seventh and sixth centuries BC, was an Etruscan town, greatly influenced by their artists and even more so by their engineers, builders of ramparts and drains.

After Tarquinius Superbus, Rome separated itself from the Etruscans, rejected the royalty and became, in 510, an aristocratic republic. The power belonged to the Senate, constituted by the heads of the Patrician families. Two consuls were elected each year; they, with the help of the quaestors who were in charge of finance, exercised absolute power. After the wars led by Rome against her neighbours and the annexation of Latium, the plebeians obtained the right to be represented by the tribunes, who were able to veto the

Ceremony in an Etruscan temple.
In the background lies a tumulus.

decisions of the Senate. The influence of the plebeian assemblies did not cease to increase.

The intellectual life, which was to make the glory of Greece, spread firstly among the Ionian towns, Greek colonies on the coast of Asia Minor, then to Lydia, realm of the wealthy Cresus. Thales of Miletus, his disciple Anaximander, Pythagoras of Samos, and Heraclitus of Ephesus consulted each other on the laws which governed nature. They formed their hypotheses on the position of the world in a harmonious universe, the theory of a world in perpetual transformation and the theory of metempsychosis.

One philosophy, of a completely different bearing, was preached in Iran, where the Persians had not yet superseded their neighbours, the Medes. In the sacred songs of the *Avesta*, Zarathustra announced a sole god, a good, just and rational creator—Ormuz. Opposed to him stood the angel of evil Ariman, against whom he led an incessant fight. The choice between the two lay with man.

A greatly exalted code of ethics was to rise out of these beliefs, which mainly accounted for the tolerance of the victorious Persians towards the subjected populations.

In India, in the sixth century, Buddha, son of a raja, withdrew from his life of luxury to preach equanimity and the liberation of the individual soul from worldly illusion. The great knowledge of this young man astonished his masters.

One day, when he was helping the workers in the fields, " seeing the tender grass torn up and scattered by the plough, covered with the eggs and little ones of insects which had been killed, he was seized by a deep grief, as if he had helped to bring about the massacre of his own relations. And, seeing the labourers with their complexions withered by the dust, by the intense heat of the sun and by the wind, the most noble of men was roused by a great compassion."

He seated himself in the shade of a tree and meditated for the first time upon the grief of the world.

Meanwhile, his father had sent for him. Eventually they found him. The sun was sinking below the horizon but, the legend says, the shadow of the tree had not moved but continued to shelter the young man.

At twenty-seven, he left his family and wandered for seven years in search of Enlightenment. At Sarnath, near Banaras, he preached his first sermon. He said that the cause of suffering was desire, and in order to suppress suffering it was necessary to suppress selfish desire. Enlightenment could be reached

Themistocles

Law of the Twelve
Roman Tables

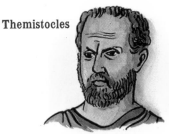

LEGES
DUODECIM
TABULARUM

SANTU MIHHLMIPC
FRIISILNLMORS
SITVRTNEPTACT
KONSVLES ROMÆ

ERAT FSMONIAN
DVODECIM TABVL
IÆ GVE IDEM IN H
ABEMVS EVNDIM

Athenian woman

Attic vase

Acropolis at Sparta

BELOW: Ritual dance of a maenad in honour of Dionysius, painted on an ancient Greek table.

ABOVE: Route of Persian invasions: in 492 BC, solid line; in 490 BC, broken line; in 480 BC, dotted line. The letter x indicates the battle grounds.

BELOW: Doric temple at Selinus in Sicily. Sicily and southern Italy abound in relics of the Greek civilisation.

Etruscan fresco in the Tomb of Leopards at Tarquinia. The Etruscans honoured the dead and, like the Egyptians, have left us rich tombs adorned with sculptures and precious paintings and enclosing numerous works of handicraftsmen. We know little about these people except that they had attained a degree of refined civilisation and of great power. When their writing is wholly deciphered the many mysteries which surround them will disappear.

BELOW: The Cerveteri tomb, called "Tomb of Reliefs!" ON THE RIGHT: A detail from a sarcophagus called the "The Married Couple!" BELOW: A bronze helmet, sword and greave from the museum at Tarquinia.

Acropolis at Athens

Pericles

Greek actors with masks and buskins

Greek sculptor

An Athenian feasting

by following the Eightfold Path which would bring right views, right motive, right speech, right action, right livelihood, right effort, right concentration and right contemplation.

It was not sufficient to have faith. Those who sought Enlightenment must destroy any selfish motives within themselves. Enlightenment, said the Buddha, could be attained by any man who strove long enough and hard enough. Hundreds of millions of men practise Buddhism in Asia today.

China lived under a feudal régime. A complicated and elaborate ceremonial ruled the habits and customs of the princely courts. The lords engaged themselves in jousting matches and in poetry tournaments. It was also the time of the sages.

Lao-tse taught that man must give himself up to the great Tao, which represents universal harmony, and thus he would regain happiness.

Then came Confucius, the most famous of Chinese philosophers. He taught, with good sense and humour, the practice of the four virtues: equity, generosity, the observance of rites, and the discrimination between Good and Evil.

The influence of this philosophy, which combined the contradictory principles of tradition and free thought, exercises itself in China even to this day.

Of central and western Europe one knows only that the Celts changed their place of residence, in about 650 BC, from south-west Germany to France. About the year 500 the Germans began to migrate, moving from the north and travelling south towards the Rhine.

At this time the whole of the East was undergoing the influence of the Persians, who were founding their empire. Having ejected the Medes, these Aryans left with Cyrus to conquer Babylon—the liberated Hebrews returned to Jerusalem—advancing as far as India, Egypt and Croesus' Lydia.

The Greek towns of Iona fell into their power. Darius gave his empire a steady administrative constitution. He built and beautified palaces in Susa and Persepolis, which Ionian and Babylonian artists came to decorate. He then conducted attacks on continental Greece. He seized Thrace and Macedonia and, due to the revolt of the Ionian cities, destroyed Miletus.

In 490, he launched an expedition against Athens which failed at Marathon, where they were defeated by a small Athenian army under the command of Miltiades. The invasion had been prevented.

Pheidippides ran to Athens, carrying the news of victory, but, on arrival, he

28

Socrates surrounded by his disciples

Discobolus

Greek slaves

Plato

A Celt conquering a Roman

died from his exertions. This spectacular feat is commemorated today in the marathon race, the chief one being at the Olympic Games, where the course is of a similar distance to that between Marathon and Athens, approximately 25 miles.

Darius died shortly afterwards. His son, Xerxes, decided to reap a brilliant revenge on the Greeks. Why should he, the Greek king, whose dominion stretched as far as India, where Buddha had just died, tolerate having been repelled by the militia of a few small Greek cities?

He armed a sizeable fleet comprising 1,200 triremes. His army was formidable; indeed none like it has ever been seen in the history of the Ancient World. The Greek historian, Herodotus, claims that the force of combatants reached 2,641,000, but he is certainly exaggerating: 360,000 is a far more probable number.

While Xerxes gathered this enormous collection of ships and infantry, what were the Greeks doing? As usual they were arguing. They fined Miltiades, the victor of Marathon, fifty talents (approximately £10,000) because he had believed that anything was permissible for a national hero. Aristides wanted the Greeks to form an army of foot soldiers. Themistocles argued that the Greek ramparts were on the water and that it was necessary to build some triremes. Although the Athenians had nicknamed Aristides 'the Just,' Themistocles succeeded in having him ostracised.

Athens raised an appeal for the union of all Greek cities. Sparta, with the confederacy of which she was head in the Pelopponesus, alone replied to the appeal. The Greeks were only going to be able to match 100,000 men against 360,000 and 380 triremes against 1,200. The situation became even more threatening because the Carthaginians were to attack, simultaneously, Sicily and southern Italy.

In the spring of 480 the Persian army crossed the Hellespont by means of a bridge of boats. They encountered the Greeks in the mountain pass of Thermopylae.

This pass lay between Mt. Oeta and the Maliac Gulf and provided the only route for an army from northern to southern Greece. The narrow pass was defended by an army of 6,000 led by Leonidas, king of Sparta. The pass was successfully held for two days, but then a traitor showed Xerxes another path over the mountains and the Persians renewed their attacks from the rear.

Leonidas and his army, consisting mostly of Spartans, were completely wiped out and the victorious Persians moved on and invaded Attica.

The Greek theatre at Epidaurus, work of Polykleitos the Younger, as it appears today. This theatre was composed of semicircular tiers where the spectators stood: it had an orchestra pit, a central space reserved for the choir, and a long, narrow, rectangular platform which formed the stage. (See also the Roman theatre Page 38.) The decoration in stonework resembled the front of a temple or of a palace. There were never more than three, exceptionally four, actors on the stage at any one time. They wore the traditional masks, which also served to amplify the voice.

BELOW: View by night of the ruins of the Acropolis at Athens. On this rock stand the Propylaea, the temple of victorious Athena, the Erechtheum, erected by Pericles, and the Parthenon, built by Ictinus and Callicrates (447-432) and decorated by the famous sculptor, Phidias.

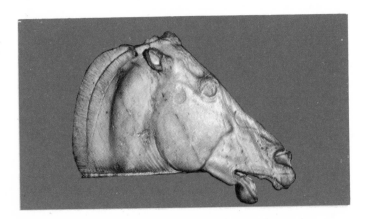

ABOVE: **Hermes and Dionysus, work of Praxiteles in 340 BC**

BELOW: **Detail from the frieze at the Parthenon, work of Phidias.**

RIGHT: **Vase decorated with an effigy of the muse of music playing the zither. The muses were the deities who presided over the arts.**

Alexander wins victory over the king of the Persians

Hippocrates

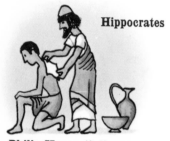

Philip II negotiating
with the Greeks

Aristotle

Palace of the Persian kings

The Greek triremes withdrew to the strait of Salamis opposite Athens. The Persian vessels would be unable to attack them there. Between the island of Salamis and the coast the channel was little more than 1¼ miles wide and it was obstructed by a little rocky promontory.

The Spartan admiral, Eurybiades, wanted to withdraw the fleet towards Pelopponesus and wait for the Persians at the isthmus of Corinth. Themistocles was opposed to the idea. His triremes had been constructed to defend Athens and they would defend it.

While the Greeks contended with each other the Persian fleet came to anchorage, blockading the bay of Salamis.

The Persians entered Athens and set fire to it. The refugees hurried to the shore and crowded into the boats which ran a shuttle service to and from the island. The dogs, who had followed their masters and who were pushed away by the sailors from the already over-laden boats, howled on the shore. The dog belonging to Pericles' father leapt into the water behind the boat which carried his master and, as told by Plutarch, died of exhaustion on reaching the island.

The military leaders blamed Themistocles for the disaster. He calmly revealed his plan. The naval battle was to be carried out in the narrow stretch of water where the large Persian ships would be hampered. To accomplish this it would be necessary to make the Persians think that the Greeks were going to flee so that they would attack.

He had no sooner spoken than a fiery officer rushed at him, his hand raised, calling him a coward. Themistocles coolly replied, " Strike, but listen."

But the assembly did not want to listen, so Themistocles took a decision which, in the event of defeat, would have cost him his life and his honour. He sent a messenger to secretly warn Xerxes that the Greeks were preparing to escape and that the moment had come to crush them.

And so it was that the Persian fleet advanced.

A song rose up from the shores of Salamis. " Sons of Greece, it is the supreme battle. Go, deliver your country, deliver your children, your women, the temples of the paternal gods and the tombs of your ancestors." It was the Greek sailors' song of triumph.

The Persian ships presented themselves in closed ranks, and, owing to their great numbers, became impeded in the channel. The Greeks charged the heavy, hampered ships. The oars of the Persian ships dashed against each other and broke. The hulls became uncontrollable and overturned. Other ships advanced to take their place and became entangled in the wrecks. The

Port and lighthouse, Alexandria

triremes of the Greeks, agile as they were, bit into these paralysed beasts and the sailors jumped into the sea.

With their oars, the Greeks beat to death the ' barbarians ' who tried to swim. '' As if they were tunny fish,'' said Eschyles, a combatant of the battle of Salamis. And in the twilight of 29th September, 480, '' a wail, mingled with sobs, alone reigned in the sea''. Eschyles was to extract the moral from that day: '' Immoderation bears the fruits of misfortune. Remember Athens and Greece. Zeus, appointed avenger of too proud thoughts, makes one pay dearly for them.''

The meeting of Alexander and Diogenes

Xerxes, when withdrawing, had left some troops on the mainland in Thessaly. The Greek infantry, led by the Spartan king, Pausanias, defeated them at Plataea the following year. Meanwhile the last Persian squadron was destroyed at Mycale, completing the Greek victory.

As for the Carthaginians who had landed in Sicily, they were attacked by surprise and successfully beaten.

Themistocles and Aristides rebuilt Athens and connected it to the port of Piraeus by long, fortified walls. They brought the Ionian islands in the confederacy of Delos under the control of Athens.

But the Athenians did not like great men and the glory of Themistocles *was* great. They had banished Miltiades, victor of the Marathon. His son, Cimon, led a campaign against Themistocles and accused him of plotting with Pausanias, who had undertaken secret negotiations with the Persians.

Alexander's sarcophagus

Pausanias, victor of Plataea, accused of having betrayed his country, was summoned to Sparta and executed. Themistocles was banished and had no alternative but to wander from city to city before going to ask for the hospitality of the king of Persia, who generously granted it to him.

Cimon, in turn, led the war against the Persians and won victory over them at the River Eurymedon in Asia Minor.

In 461, Cimon was accused of treason because he had helped the Spartans to quell a revolt of their helots. Pericles had him banished.

In Rome, in the same era, the common people strengthened their rights. About 451, the Law of the Twelve Tables was proclaimed, engraved in marble and exhibited in the Forum, in order that those citizens who were able could read it. This was the first written Roman law.

Then the plebeians gained recognition for the validity of marriages between the patricians and the plebeians. Later the consulship itself was to be open to the plebeians.

Slowly but surely the Romans expanded their domain and shook off the yoke

Diagram of the construction of the Appian Way

	8-16 inches of basalt
	12 inches of medium-sized gravel
	18 inches of large gravel
	8 inches of small gravel

Roman soldiers

Audacious and irresistible,
spurring his horse
Bucephalus into a
thousand battles,
Alexander the Great
had the talent
to co-ordinate
heavy infantry
and light cavalry.
He made use of
catapults and other
war machines
with great efficacy.

The empire of Alexander the Great, with the routes of his expeditions. The Macedonian enterprise marked the meeting of the western and eastern civilisations.

OPPOSITE LEFT: The legendary Macedonian hero, conqueror of Darius III, became a character of Persian mythology, as this miniature, representing the death of Alexander, shows.

Salonica

BLACK SEA

CASPIAN SEA

Balkh

Adana

Tehran

MEDITERRANEAN SEA

PERSIAN EMPIRE

Susa

Alexandria

Babylon

Persepolis

RED SEA

PERSIAN GULF

ARABIAN SEA

The Great Wall of China

Carthaginian possessions in 264 BC

Hannibal

Elephant prepared for battle

Archimedes

of the Etruscans, to whom their civilisation owed so much; for example, the atrium of houses, the semicircular arch, the theatre and the games of the circus.

Thirteen miles from Rome the opulent city of Veies still shone over Italy, like Athens in Greece. The Romans succeeded in taking the city in 396 and burnt it. It was Rome henceforth which was to shine over Italy.

Pericles dominated the political life of Athens from 467 to 429. But it was not until the end of 449, when the Greeks signed the peace of Callias with the Persians, that the Greek ' miracle ' was realised. One saw then, although not for a long time, order and liberty living in harmony.

Pericles exercised democracy while exerting a wise and balanced personal power.

He allowed the poorest citizens to serve in the high offices of State. In order to allow them to perform their duties, he gave a daily indemnity to members of the boule and the ekklesia, to the magistrates of the heliaia and to all office holders. He invited the rich to partake in the rule of the State, but limited the rights of citizenship to men born of Greek parents, without forbidding the aliens the right to take an active part in the prosperity of Athens. The slaves spared the citizens the trouble of having to undertake manual labour and allowed them the freedom of mind which they greatly treasured.

The balance established by Pericles secured for Athens an unprecedented intellectual and artistic progress.

The theatre, which was really invented by the Greeks, reached its highest standard. Aeschylus tells in the *Oresteia* the misfortunes of the Atrides. Sophocles shows in *Antigone*, *Oedipus Tyrannus*, and *Oedipus at Colonus* the misfortune of amazing heroes in the grips of implacable fate.

Euripides, the most modern of the three, rejected heavenly alibis and showed man responsible for himself, for his passions, for his greatness and his wretchedness. His most beautiful works are *Alcestis*, *Medea*, and *Iphigenia in Tauris*.

Aristophanes was soon to introduce satire into the theatre. The great lyric poet, Pindar, introduced the pastoral theme. Herodotus and Thucydides told of the wars of the Medes and, later, unfortunately, the wars of the Peloponnesians.

Philosophy flourished in Athens. The sophists developed a positivist philosophy, but through their tendency towards over-clever reasoning, it

36

Roman port

Part of the altar
at Pergamum

The Cimbri moving southwards

declined. Socrates reacted by charging man to judge himself in order that he might reach accuracy of thought and action. His critical mind caused him to be accused of inciting the young people towards atheism and he was condemned to death. He spent his last days in prison, advising his friends, and died peacefully in 399, drinking the hemlock brought to him by the jailer.

Pericles died of the plague in 429, at a time when Greek sculpture and architecture had reached their heights. The monuments of the Acropolis in Athens, constructed at Pericles' command, are the most magnificent evidence of this genius: the Parthenon with its frieze of the Athenians on their way to a festival in honour of their goddess, Athena; the Propylaea, and the statue of Athena Parthenos by Phidias, the greatest sculptor of the time.
Other great sculptors of this time were Polyclitus and Myron, whose famous statue, the Discobolus, we still admire today.
At the time when Pericles died, the perpetual rivalry of the Greek cities broke out into a fratricidal war, the war of the Peloponnesus. Sparta formed a coalition of the mercantile cities against the confederacy of Delos, which had been subordinated to Athens.

In 421, the peace of Nicias brought a short truce, soon to be broken by a brilliant man, although one who was little mindful of his responsibilities, Alcibiades, who led an expedition against Syracuse, ally of Sparta and of Corinth. The expedition ended in disaster for the Athenian fleet.
In 404, the Spartans, supported by the Persians, won a decisive victory near Aegospotami, where Lysander captured the great bulk of the Athenian fleet. This final defeat brought about the end of the hegemony of Athens and of the confederacy of Delos, but the supremacy of Sparta did not last long.
Theban Epaminondas put an end to it in 371 and substituted, for a time, that of Thebes. The real beneficiary of the struggle between the Greek cities was the Persian empire which regained the Greek towns on the coast of Asia Minor.
The decadence of Greece in the fourth century was purely political. Its civilisation maintained its brilliance, of which the doctor Hippocrates, the sculptors Scopas, Praxiteles, and Lysippus are all evidence. Although Socrates had been condemned to drink hemlock, Plato spread his ideas, while adding to them his own. In his famous Academy he taught that reality was eternal and changeless, and that the soul was immortal. He maintained that men could only gain true knowledge, as opposed to opinions based on perceptions

Lucius Cornelius Sulla

Revolt of Spartacus

A section of the Appian Way which joined Rome with Brindisi, a great port opening onto Greece and the East. It was constructed partly by the censor Claudius Appius (312 BC). The construction of roads was, for the Romans, the prelude to the conquest of a region.

BELOW: The theatre at Leptis Magna (Libya), ancient town on the northern coast of Africa, built by the Phoenicians and colonised by the Romans.

View of the ruins of the Roman forum, vital centre of the city, and site of the temples and of the most important public buildings. The arch with the three porticos, which can be seen on the right, was erected by the emperor Septimus Severus. In the background lies the palace of the Senate, constructed in the Middle Ages on the site of the ancient Tabularium where the public archives were kept: this is now the site of the Town Hall in Rome.

BELOW, FROM LEFT TO RIGHT: A Gallic hunter, the consul Marius, Lucius Cornelius Sulla, Julius Caesar. Contrary to the Greeks, the Romans did not represent people idealistically but with realism. They sought to capture the characteristic features of each individual, whether by accentuating the details of the face or by ensuring that the expression reflected the personality. In their ardent respect for the individual, the Romans remained faithful to the artistic tradition of the Etruscans.

Caesar supervises the construction of the bridge over the Rhine

Cleopatra

Roman bridge

Cicero

The three wise men from the East

and experiences of the changing world, if their minds could aspire from particular objects and ideas to universal ones. His dialogues, *The Banquet*, *The Republic*, *The Laws*, express his ideas on aesthetics, pedagogy and politics.

His pupil, Aristotle, disagreed with his ideas. Reality, he said, did not lie in pure thought but in actions and experience. Knowledge, he said, was accurate observation of actions. On this, and only this, must logical reason be founded. He believed that one element of the soul was eternal— Reason.

Whilst Plato and Aristotle philosophised, the blonde giants of the Celtic race, the Gauls, moved south into Italy where the Etruscans, weakened by Rome, could not oppose their advance. Nine years after the destruction of Veies, in 387, the Gauls, having ravaged Etruria, arrived before the ramparts of Rome. The geese in the Capitol gave the alert during the night and the Romans hastened to the ramparts and repelled the attack of the Gauls. The latter did not leave Italy but dwelt in the north, in what was called Cisalpine Gaul.

Aristotle said, '' Since intelligence is the highest virtue, the first duty of the State is not to drag down the citizens under a military superiority but to raise them in order that they will make a just usage of peace.''

And Aristotle's pupil was called Alexander. Alexander's father, King Philip of Macedonia, seeing the anarchy into which the Greek cities had fallen, had undertaken to bring them together under his authority.

He had formed a strong army: an infantry made up of Macedonian peasants, armed with swords and sixteen-feet long spears; a battering artillery with catapults; and lastly, a great innovation, the Companions of the King, about 800 feudal barons constituting a cavalry.

In Athens, a great orator named Demosthenes clamoured for the return to civic virtues. He succeeded in rousing the Athenians and the Thebans against the Macedonians.

The encounter took place in the plain of Chaeronea on 1st September, 338. At the end of a fierce battle the young Alexander, hardly eighteen, showed at the head of the cavalry to what temerity his courage could carry him. A thousand Athenians had been killed, two thousand taken prisoner, and the ' sacred battalion ' of Thebans, three hundred men, perished to the very last man.

Philip was now supreme and, at the head of a united Greece, he prepared to

Triumph of a victorious general returning to Rome

Atrium in a Patrician house

make an assault on the Persian empire. But this was to be the work of his son, for Philip was assassinated in 336. In 334, Alexander took up the Persian project begun by his father and commenced a brilliant, eleven-year career, during which time he was to bring Greek civilisation as far as the Indus.

Unfortunately, Alexander died of malaria in 323, at Babylon, the city which he wanted to make the capital of his empire. Immediately, risings were precipitated in Greece, but they were soon suppressed by the Macedonians under the leadership of the regent, Antipater.

Rome, having subjected central Italy, attacked the Greek cities of the south. Pyrrhus—with the use of elephants, to which the Roman horses were not accustomed—defeated the Romans at Heraclea and Asculum. But these victories were won at great cost, indeed they were of a kind to which his name has been attributed—Pyrrhic victories.

In 264, Italy was unified from the Arno and the Rubicon to the Strait of Messina, and Rome found itself in direct rivalry with Carthage.

Carthage had established its settlements in Spain, Sardinia and Sicily. In 264, the Romans crossed the Strait of Messina and seized Syracuse and Agrigento. Carthage reacted immediately under the leadership of Hamilcar.

It was the first Punic War. The Romans won two naval victories, in 260 and 241, and Sicily became the first Roman province. The Roman legions had ventured for the first time outside Italian territory. Nothing could stop them now.

Each of the two countries reformed its forces. Hamilcar occupied Spain and Rome expanded its territories in the plain of Po. The Flaminian Way, which ran northwards through the Apennine Mountains to Ariminum, was constructed. In 221, Rome set foot in Illyria and established its protectorate even in Epirus.

Roman amphora

Roman peasant woman in front of aqueduct

In China, after the period of the decline of imperial power and the increase of feudalism, marked by wars of atrocious cruelty, the realm of Ch'in undertook to subjugate its neighbours. In 246, the king, like Alexander, annexed with alacrity all the realms situated between Peking itself and the Blue River. He then took the title of Ch'in Shih Huang Ti and was acknowledged as emperor of all China. From Ch'in, China was to receive its name. In eleven years he organised a great empire. Shih Huang Ti is particularly remembered for the building of the Great Wall of China against the forays of the Huns of Mongolia.

Conversation between Varus and Arminius

RIGHT: **Plan of a typical house of a Roman Patrician.** The house had only one entrance opening into the Vestibulum (the two shops on either side were completely separate from the house and were rented). The Vestibulum led to the Atrium, a large reception room into which light passed through a rectangular opening in the middle of the ceiling. A pool of the same dimensions, the Impluvium, was situated underneath the opening to collect the rain water. Several small rooms opened off the Atrium. The most important rooms were the Tablinum, where the head of the family resided, and the Triclinium, or dining-room. The rear of the house was comprised of the Peristylium, a sort of cloister providing a covered walk around a garden, onto which opened other rooms, more pleasant because they were away from the noise.

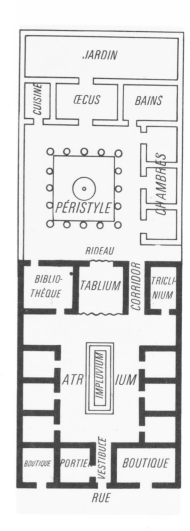

Not all Romans lived in houses as sumptuous as that shown in the plan, with gardens like those photographed in the top picture above of a house in Pompei, or paved with splendid mosaics. A detail from the mosaics in the Piazza Armerina in Sicily is pictured right. Those less fortunate Romans contented themselves with far more modest dwellings, without gardens and baths. The houses, several storeys high, were constructed of more economical material, such as loam, like the house at Herculaneum (pictured above). Families often rented a flat in a house of five or six storeys. In these tenements, the ground floor apartments were considered luxurious because they had, at their disposal, running water and drains. The number of these common houses was naturally greater than the number of private houses.

Model of a Roman anchor. When the Romans, landlubbers as they were, became fearless sailors, they improved the system of anchorage in order to be able to use it in the open seas.

BELOW: Aqueduct over the River Gard, tributary of the Rhône, near Nîmes. The Romans solved the problem of feeding water to the towns by building constructions similar to this masterpiece of ingenuity, constructed in 19 BC. The channel, about six feet wide, which brought the water to the city of Gard, was supported by three superimposed bridges. The lower bridge is still used today.

Eruption of Vesuvius

Emperor Nero

St. Sebastian the martyr

Destruction of Jerusalem

Germanic dwelling

In the West the second Punic War (218—201) was to put Rome on the brink of its downfall.

It was led from the Carthaginian coast by Hamilcar's son, Hannibal, one of the greatest leaders in history. Deciding to wage war in the territory of Italy itself, he crossed Spain, the Pyrénées, and then crossed the Alps into northern Italy with his elephants. Soaring from victory to victory, he wiped out the Roman legions at Lake Trasimene, then at Cannae, where 45,000 Romans were killed and 20,000 taken prisoner. Rome seemed lost. And yet, it was when most threatened that Rome was able to give of its best.

When Hannibal arrived before the walls which had been built against the Gauls, he found them decorated with wild defenders. He did not attack, but made his army return towards the south where it slumbered peacefully.

Rome took advantage of this rest and turned its attention towards the town of Syracuse. For three years the town defended itself, thanks to the mathematician Archimedes, whose war machines flung enormous stones on to the Roman infantry. Eventually Syracuse was occupied by surprise. It was the Roman's turn to settle down in enemy territory.

The consul Scipio, after having conquered Spain, landed in Africa. In 202, at Zama, he, who was to be called ' the African ', overwhelmed Hannibal's army, which fled.

The settled peace in 201 gave Rome control of the western Mediterranean, but Carthage rose again. '' It is necessary to destroy Carthage,'' Cato cried incessantly. His wish was to be granted in 146 after the victory of Scipio Aemilianus, adopted grandson of ' the African '.

Certain Hellenistic states having supported Carthage, Rome looked towards the Greek world. In 197, the Macedonian king, Philip V, was conquered by the consul Flaminius, who proclaimed the freedom of the Greek cities.

In 190, the victory over the king of Syria drove the Seleucids from Asia Minor. In order to stress the downfall of the Seleucids, Rome promoted the reconstitution of a Jewish state under the Maccabees.

In 171, Macedonia attacked Greece. Its king, Perseus, was beaten at Pydna. After a last uprising in 148 Macedonia became a Roman province. In 146, the year of the burning of Carthage, Corinth was destroyed and the subjugated Greece became the Roman province of Achaea.

In 133, the king of Pergamum died and bequeathed his kingdom to the Romans.

During all these conquests, Greek culture had captivated the Romans to

The Baptism of Constantine

The Black Gate at Trier

Hadrian's Wall

Making paper in China

Life within the confines of the Roman Empire

such an extent that they plundered numerous works of art and brought with them to Rome many scientists, philosophers and historians, such as Polybius.

Meanwhile, in Rome, a period of social agitation had begun. The peasant population had been impoverished by the wars and the formation of large estates. A new class threatened to assert itself, that of the knights who had been enriched by the conquest. To remedy the situation, Tiberius Gracchus, tribune of the plebeians, proposed in 133 to limit the landed properties. The senators had him assassinated. Ten years after they were to drive his brother, Caius, to suicide because, allying himself with the knights, he had distributed the lands and reduced the price of corn.

The victories of Marius in Numidia, and over the Cimbri and the Teutons, who threatened the frontiers north of the Roman world, were not to convince the senators of his wisdom. Marius was refused land for his legionaries. The whole of Italy revolted, in spite of the tardy decision of the Senate to grant the right of citizenship to all Italians. The unrest lasted some years, causing countless disturbances.

The patrician Sulla, a former lieutenant to Marius, distinguished himself and entered into conflict with his former general, supported by the popular party. The civil war reached Rome itself. Sulla was to put an end to it on his return from Asia where he had gone to make war against Mithridates, king of Pontus. In 82, he established himself as dictator.

Sulla began ridding himself of enemies by banishing them. Then he modified the institutions, reduced the rights of the knights and the tribunes of the plebeians, and strengthened the Senate. After his retreat from public life and his death, in 78 BC, these noble reforms did not last long, for they were opposed by ambitious generals who supported the people.

These generals were called upon to reduce the revolt of Sertorius in Spain and to oppose Mithridates, who rekindled the war in the Orient. This was done by Pompey, who crowned himself with glory by pacifying Spain, by eliminating the pirates of the Mediterranean and by conquering Mithridates. In Asia he organised the provinces of Pontus, Syria and Cilicia (66—62 BC).

In Italy, in 71, another general, named Crassus, had overcome, at the end of two years, the revolt of the slaves led by Spartacus. This revolt, unique in the ancient world—for it brought to question the very basis of the economic system—made Spartacus the forerunner of our modern revolutionaries. The repression was to be terrible. For example, at the command of the conqueror, six thousand slaves were crucified along the Appian Way.

In Rome conspiracies took the place of plots.

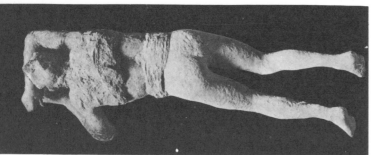

A street in Pompei with pavements and crossings for pedestrians made up of high stepping stones which prevented them from dirtying their footwear. The chariot wheels passed through the broad gaps in the stones.

LEFT: A Pompeian killed during the eruption of Vesuvius in 79 AD. The cast was obtained by pouring liquid plaster into the imprint made by the body in the soft lava.

Ruins of the Colosseum in Rome, which was the amphitheatre of Flavius. Arenas like this one were capable of holding 87,000 spectators.

BELOW: The Arch of Titus, built after the war against the Jews to celebrate the Emperor's victory and the destruction of Jerusalem. Emperors erected these arches all over the Empire, tangible proof of the power of the Caesars and Rome.

The burial of a Germanic king

Division of the Roman Empire

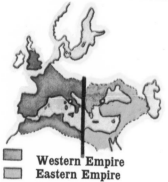

■ Western Empire
■ Eastern Empire

Attila

The Huns in Rome

Mausoleum of Theodoric at Ravenna

In 63, the greatest advocate of Rome, Marcus Tullius Cicero, partisan of the traditional republic, defeated without any proof, but by sole virtue of his eloquence, the conspiracy of Catiline against the republic.

In 60, Pompey returned to Rome in all his glory, but not daring to take the dictatorship. He allied himself, in a secret agreement, with Crassus and with a patrician who had regularly found himself amongst the *cursus honorum*, those who held many important offices, without bringing himself to the attention of the Romans. His name was Julius Caesar. This was the first triumvirate.

In 59, Caesar, as consul, distributed the lands amongst the veterans of Pompey. Then he appointed himself proconsul of the two provinces nearest to Gaul, whilst Pompey became proconsul of Spain and Crassus went to war against the Parthians.

Caesar took advantage of the local disturbances in Gaul to undertake the conquest which was to open to him the road to power. He defeated the Helvetians, driving them back into Switzerland, chased the Germans back across the Rhine and out of Gaul, and subdued the entire north of the country. He was so successful that, in 52, there was a national revolt under the great Gallic leader, Vercingetorix. This great chief, despite his bravery and his sense of organisation, did not have the means to defeat the Roman efficiency, and it was at the siege of Alesia that he was forced to surrender to Caesar. Gaul was to be Roman.

In Rome, where disorder reigned, the republic put itself in the hands of Pompey, who changed parties and took the side of the Senate. Crassus died in the East, in 53, where his legions had led an unsuccessful war against the Parthians in Asia.

Pompey became alarmed by Caesar's success and, in 49, he allied himself with the conservatives and Caesar was ordered to give up his army.

The struggle between the two former allies was to be brief. Refusing to surrender, Caesar, with his army, crossed the Rubicon in December 50 BC, and entered Rome. Pompey fled to the Balkans where Caesar overwhelmed him at Pharsalus in Thessaly, 48 BC. He pursued him into Egypt, where he found that Pompey had been assassinated.

Caesar decided to stay in Alexandria, glory of the Hellenistic civilisation, where he met and fell in love with Cleopatra. In two years, Caesar subdued Pompey's partisans in the East, in Africa and in Spain. Before returning to Rome, in 45, he made Cleopatra ruler of Egypt.

On reaching Rome the people granted him the powers of dictator for life.

The Baptism of Clovis at Rheims

Emperor Justinian

Saint Benedict

He refused the crown offered to him by Mark Antony, but he had all the powers of a king. He had supreme power over the army, the tribune and over the censorship of customs.

He did not relinquish these powers until his assassination in 44 BC. His decisions as statesman were as rapid as his military victories. He distributed lands to the veterans, reorganised the administration of the provinces, conferred widely the right of citizenship and undertook extensive travels. With the astronomer, Alexandria Sosigenes, Caesar introduced the Julian calendar.

But the traditionalist party had not said its last word. On the eve of his departure for the great expedition he had planned to the East, he was assassinated by a group of senators. The leaders of these conspirators were Cassius and Brutus.

Cicero abolished the dictatorship and delivered his violent speeches, the *Philippics*, against Cæsar's Lieutenant, Mark Antony.

Antony allied himself with Caesar's great-nephew, Octavian, and with Marcus Lepidus, who had also served under Caesar. This second triumvirate began by banishing the enemies of Caesar. Cicero was killed, his head and his right hand displayed on the rostrums of the forum.

Then Octavian and Antony crushed Brutus and Cassius at Philippi in Macedonia, 42 BC. Antony took command of the East, where, after his meeting with Cleopatra, whom he married, he regarded himself as king. He gave Cleopatra and her children large parts of the eastern provinces, which enraged his supporters in Rome. Antony was divested of his authority. He and Octavian became rivals.

While civil war once again threatened Rome, Octavian destroyed the navy of his adversary in the bay of Actium in Greece. The fallen hero committed suicide.

Egypt became a Roman province and Octavian became master of the whole empire. Roman peace was to reign over the Mediterranean world for two centuries.

At the other extremity of Asia another peace corresponded to that of Rome—the Chinese peace. In 202, the Han dynasty was founded, its greatest representative being the Emperor Wu-ti. After several successful wars against the Huns he spread his protectorate over the caravan routes as far as Russian Turkestan. As he was 'Son of the Heavens', the emperor took possession

Mohammed

The Koran

ABOVE: The central courtyard of the Abbey of Monte Cassino built to replace the modest monastery, founded by Saint Benedict on the same site in 529 AD. The new building replaces the original one which was destroyed in 1944 during the Second World War.

ABOVE, RIGHT: Mohammed blessing the Black Stone of Mecca, in an Arab painting of the 14th century. The Black Stone, a meteorite, had already been an object of worship before Islam. It was venerated by the Moslems, who saw it as an angel condemned by his sins to remain in that form until the day of the Last Judgement.

LEFT: The palace of Theodoric, from a mosaic in the church of Sant' Apollinaire Nuovo at Ravenna.

RIGHT: The famous basilica of Saint Sophia in Constantinople, a masterpiece of Byzantine architecture. Built by Justinian, between 532 and 537 AD, it was made into a mosque by the Turks after they took Byzance in 1453.

50

The Mosque of Cordoba

The invention of porcelain

Battle of Poitiers

Monogram of Charlemagne

Crowning of Charlemagne

of all the land in China. He spread the principles of Confucius and organised teaching according to those doctrines.

The successors of Wu-ti put an end to the claims of the Western Huns for five centuries. The Empire of the Han dynasty developed scholarship and culture to a high degree.

In Rome, Gaius Octavianus became the *Princeps*, first citizen of Rome, in 27 BC. He adopted the name Augustus and seized all power to himself; he is regarded as the first Roman Emperor. With the help of his friends, Agrippa and Tiberius, he began to reorganise the Empire from top to bottom. The administration of Rome was carried out by the Prefects who were subordinate only to the Emperor. The Prefect of the Praetorium, commander of the army, had the most important task.

Augustus created senatorial and equestrian order and defined the hierarchy of the different social classes. The ancient provinces were entrusted to the Proconsul, the newer ones to the Legates. Rome became that marble city which is now praised so much. The architects and sculptors, without attaining the perfection of the Greeks, nevertheless produced works of real splendour, such as the altars of the Peace of Augustus.

The provinces, like Italy, laid roads and built bridges, aqueducts and baths. The century of Augustus saw the emergence of new poets.

At the beginning of the century, the poet Catullus and the historian Sallustus enhanced Roman literature. Later came Virgil, the political poet of Augustus, who wrote the *Georgics*, *Bucolics* and the *Aeneid*, an epic poem about the foundation of Rome. Livy wrote a superb history of Rome.

This was also the time of Propertius and Horace, the great poets, and Ovid, who was victim of the strict rules of the time.

The only failure of Augustus, which was to have heavy consequences, was his inability to conquer the Germans. The country had been overcome by Tiberius and Drusus but, in the year 9 AD, the revolt of Arminius pushed back the frontier of the Empire to the Rhine. In central Europe it was marked by the Danube.

Augustus died in 14 AD, leaving to his successors the most powerful empire in the world. Rome, the Eternal City, was now the admiration of both East and West.

In Judea, one of the countries annexed by Rome, Jesus was born five or six years before the year we take as the first of the Christian era.

Imperial Frankish palace

Carolingian church at Germiny-des-Prés

The first successors of Augustus, his relatives, maintained the Empire; but their rule is marked by bloody family feuds and by the first interventions of the Praetors.

During the reign of the cruel Nero a fire destroyed part of Rome. The people blamed the Emperor. Scapegoats had to be found and so the Christians were accused. The first martyrs died, torn to pieces in the arenas by wild beasts, while the Roman spectators looked on in amusement. Or they were smeared with oil, crucified and then set fire to, so as to illuminate the road down which the Emperor travelled.

Who were these brave Christians? Often they were slaves or men and women of poor class who listened to the stories of the Jews, who told them that Jesus, the Son of God, had come on the earth. In Galilee He had preached of poverty, of love of one's neighbour, of faith in a just God and an eternal life. He died on a cross in Jerusalem " to redeem the sins of the world " Three days later He rose from the dead and after rejoining His Father in Heaven, He ordained His disciples, saying " Go and teach all nations."

This new faith was preached in Rome by the apostle Peter, who had followed his master across Palestine, and by a respected Jewish scholar and Roman knight, Paul of Tarsus. Together with the twelve apostles, Paul was a great propagator of the Christian faith. This Hellenist Jew, who spoke in the synagogues, the market places of Greek cities and the suburbs of Rome, understood that all men, not only the Chosen People, would be saved by faith in Christ the Redeemer. His Epistles provided sustenance for all Christianity. He was beheaded in Rome about 64 AD and Saint Peter was crucified.

Frankish warrior of about 800 AD

The Viking city of Haithabu

From 69 to 96 AD the Flavian dynasty gave Rome four Emperors. During the reign of Titus, the cities of Pompei and Herculaneum were buried by an eruption of the volcano Vesuvius. Tacitus wrote his *Annals* and *Histories*.

With the Antonines, the title of ' princeps ' was not hereditary. The prince chose his own successor from the most stoic of candidates.

During the reign of Trajan (96—117 AD) the Roman Empire saw a great expansion, with the annexing of Dacia, north of the Danube, and the victories against the Parthians. Trajan took the Roman. Eagle as far as the Indian Ocean.

However, this was short-lived success, for, after Trajan's death, Hadrian fixed the boundary of the Empire at the Euphrates. Hadrian (117—138 AD) spent a lot of his reign travelling through the Empire, where the riches of the

Viking warship

BELOW: The cathedral at Aachen, a masterpiece of Carolingian architecture. The central part was made up of the Palatine Chapel, which Charlemagne built from the model of San Vitale in Ravenna. Charlemagne made his residence in Aachen and the town thus became the capital of the Carolingian Empire. The territory of the state was subdivided into counties and grouped into electoral districts watched over by the ' missi dominici '. The Emperor made the laws, submitting them to assemblies of lords who met twice a year.

ABOVE, LEFT AND RIGHT: Two T'ang ceramics of a polo player and a camel. During the reign of the T'ang dynasty China was reunified and reached the height of its artistic power. Besides ceramics, which were largely exported, religious and landscape painters achieved much success. Poetry became popular with the efforts of Li Po and Tu Fu.

BELOW: Charlemagne crowned, a large sword in his right hand and the orb in his left, symbols of his power on the earth. This is a detail from an equestrian statue of the 9th century preserved in the Carnavalet Museum, Paris. Charlemagne is shown here with a great beard, as he appeared in the chronicles of the 11th century. In reality, according to his official biographer, Einhard, the Emperor did not have a beard, only a moustache. A great warrior and a skilful ruler, Charlemagne was also the promoter of farming and he founded the Palatine school.

BELOW: Some of the jewels of Queen Theodelind of Lombardy, which are preserved in the Cathedral of Monza, near Milan.

BELOW, LEFT: The famous iron crown, a Byzantine piece of the ninth century with which several kings were crowned. The Book of Gospels is a precious Oriental work given to Queen Theodelind by Gregory the Great.

Life in a monastery

Arabic and Indian numerals

A 7238467 8 9
B 123 8 96789
C 123456789

Alfred the Great

Seal of the monastery at Cluny

Henry I

provinces began to surpass those of Rome. At the end of his life he subdued the last Jewish revolt, after which nothing remained of Judea and Jerusalem. The Jews who survived this massacre then began to disperse all over the world.

The Peace of Rome ended during the reign of the philosophical Emperor Marcus Aurelius. In his book *Meditations* he counselled his readers to seek happiness in co-operation with divine reason, which he believed filled the universe. Marcus Aurelius had to struggle against Germanic tribes who tried to over-run Dacia, and also against the Parthians. The Roman legions also brought a plague back from the East which was similar in destructive power to the Black Death, and which decimated the population of Rome and of Italy itself.

During the period of the Antonines, Greek-Latin culture was furthered by such men as the historian Plutarch, the censor Appian, the philosopher Epictetus, the doctor Galen and the astronomer Ptolemy.

The Christians gained new converts in the Romans who were tired of the stories of the old Latin religion. The Christian religion first attracted the poorer classes and later the patricians. Bishops were in charge of their communities. Martyrs such as the slave Blandin at Lyons, and Cecilia in Rome, give examples of the unweakening faith.

In China, after the attempt at a socialist state by the Emperor Wang-mang, the Han dynasty regained power up to 229 AD. During the new 'Chinese Peace' several valuable inventions appeared of which paper and the compass are the most important, and which the Western world then ignored.

After the peace came anarchy and the country was divided into three kingdoms. In 280 AD the Chinese population fell from fifty-six to sixteen million people.

In 226, the Persian Empire was revived under the Sassanids who replaced the Parthian kings.

At the other end of the Roman Empire the Germans moved into Gaul. Finally the Goths came down from the Baltic to the shores of the Black Sea, harrying the frontier armies at the Danube.

In Rome itself crisis followed crisis, with devaluation and depopulation. The Illyrian Emperors attempted to right the situation. Diocletian (284—305) organised Tetrarchs to ease the defence of the frontiers. Henceforth the Empire was split into Eastern and Western parts with separate rulers for each side.

Diocletian endangered his attempts at reform by increasing the persecution

Meissen Castle

of the Christians. After him came confusion from which emerged Constantine in triumph to become the first Christian Emperor.

In 312, with an army of Germans and Gauls, Constantine left Gaul and took possession of Northern Italy. On the road to Rome he saw, according to legend, a large cross in the sky, and under it were the words in Greek: "With this sign you will conquer." He did conquer in effect and entered Rome. Constantine shared the Empire with Licinius, who took the Eastern sector. They proclaimed the Edict of Milan in 313 AD which authorised all forms of worship and Christianity became a recognised religion.

In 324 AD, Constantine seized the Orient from Licinius and had him put to death. The Empire was once again unified. The name of the capital, Byzance, was changed to Constantinople.

In 325 AD, Constantine presided over the Council of Nicaea, which condemned the heresy of Arius who held that Jesus was not the Son of God. The schism of Arius nevertheless continued to progress among the Barbarians.

Constantine was baptised and died in 337 AD. Christianity became the state religion during the reign of Theodosius (379—395), who persecuted the pagans and abolished the Olympic Games.

In 375 AD, the Huns crossed the Volga, pushing back the Goths who came into the Empire and were accepted as 'foederati' or allies, settling in Thrace. Theodosius took numerous Barbarians into the army. His best general, Stilicon, was a Vandal.

On the death of Theodosius the Empire was divided between his sons—the West to Honorius and the East to Arcadius. Waves of Barbarian invasions followed. In 401 AD, the Visigoths penetrated Italy. In 410 AD, their chief, Alaric, seized Rome. A Visigoth kingdom was installed in Aquitaine and the north of Spain. The Vandals ravaged Gaul, where the Franks lived in the north, passed into Spain and then Africa. In 430 AD, Saint Augustine died during the siege of Hippo where he was bishop.

The Burgundians took Savoy and the basin between the Saône and the Rhône. The Huns, commanded by Attila, arrived at Paris in 451 but the city held them off, thanks to Saint Genevieve. They were defeated at the battle known variously as Chalons, Troyes, or the 'Catalaunian Fields' by the joint forces of the Romans and Germans.

Attila died after a last raid in Italy in 453 AD, bringing about the end of his Empire.

Hungarian warrior

Top of a Roman column

Roman window

Otto the Great

f eft oint̄ce. facieīṣ;
ungūt̄ardī z
māima copoſitat
il inaltareſē bonī
crareē zſedolēnuṣ.
ārnauuiſtaz; uſtar
bonī op̄ṣiŝ ſinceṗt
tpuluetē zedigere
crefeṣe. &ſub aĺiā
don feſtu depigmaſſ
f bonub; con epamar
qi adſupmar. &ad
un diararaeſpmuleṣ
arraſſ incenſōr.
quemagīṣ humiĺi
efe ſub leuxauit
uaqb; delecarat.
odoſtan ſuauiſſ.
opocarlı p̄ſi leggaŕ
z luxarr coſtam
caufeu. &oſcan
emarnu arigeĺ
eoregonib; ſcōr

I B E R X V I I I.

X V I I I I.

Culaufor eft qiccrffu̅macr ut urnar
margno lærbofſqueſpriurſ æbln colando
uocarer; Druuſ ē arnaquopi
inluf duob; ſpan̄ bære pazrefe
& bære cefrefe; Culaufor arghi cimiſ afpergo.

LEFT: The facing of the High Altar in the Basilica of Saint Ambrose in Milan. This work, in silver and gold, is by a German craftsman.

BELOW, LEFT: Semicircular arches and groined vaultings formed the essential elements of Roman architecture.

BELOW: The Basilica of Saint Ambrose in Milan; one of the first examples of Roman architecture in Italy.

Groined vault.

Semicircular arch.

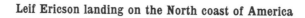
Leif Ericson landing on the North coast of America

Saint Stephen, King of Hungary

A merchant, about 1,000 AD

King Canute's empire

In 455 AD, the Vandals attacked and sacked Rome. In 476 AD, the last Emperor of the West, Romulus Augustulus, was deposed by the chief of the Barbarian mercenaries, Odoacer.

The Barbarian kingdoms divided up the debris of the Roman Empire between themselves. In the north of Gaul, in 481, the Salian Franks elected as their leader Clovis, son of their old chief.

In thirty years Clovis conquered the greater part of Gaul and was baptised a Christian at Rheims in 496 AD. His conversion was of considerable importance—it rallied to Clovis' side the Church and the Gallic-Roman population and made him the Catholic champion against the Visigoths, whom he drove back beyond the Pyrénées in 507 AD.

The sons of Clovis divided among themselves the kingdom which adjoined Burgundy, Provence and Bavaria. Their descendants, the idle kings, were to fall under the subjection of an aristocracy of great landowners.

In Italy, the Ostrogoths founded a kingdom in 493 AD. Their sovereign, Theodoric, showed wisdom that was very rare in this time of general decadence. He proclaimed himself to be the ' son and servant ' of the Emperor of the East. He kept in his service all the officials of the old Western Empire. He displayed great respect for the Senate and he supported the bishops. Reports that he divided a third of the lands of Italy between his soldiers seem to be unfounded.

Theodoric restored the Colosseum, the theatre of Pompei, the amphitheatres of Verona, Pavia and Milan. In Ravenna he built several palaces, the mausoleum of Galla Placidia and the basilica of Sant' Apollinaire Nuovo.

Theodoric once said, " It is deplorable for a Roman to imitate a Goth, but it is a wise Goth who imitates a Roman! "

Senators and men of letters declared themselves his friends. The bishop of Pavia announced his panegyric, although he was an Arian. But the Catholic Emperor Justin ascended the throne of Byzance and ordered the exclusion of all Arian functions, both military and civil, throughout the empire.

Theodoric made an appeal for reason: " To claim to dominate people's consciences is to usurp the power of God. By the very nature of things, the power of sovereigns is limited to political government. They have the right to punish only those who disturb the general public peace."

Pope John I himself travelled to Byzance to plead for tolerance. But his journey was in vain. Theodoric, who truly deserved the heritage of the

The Battle of Hastings

The Church of Saint Sophia at Kiev

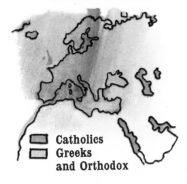

Viking inscription

Antonines, died in 526 AD, dishonoured by the Italians to whom he had wanted to give Roman order.

The opposition of the Romans and the Goths encouraged the plans of the Eastern Emperor Justinian (527—565 AD), who dreamed of re-establishing religious and imperial unity.

This absolute monarch, surrounded by very wise counsellors, of whom the most efficient was his wife Theodora, sent his generals Belisarius and Narses to re-occupy Africa, Italy and the south-west of Spain. Only the Frankish kingdom escaped from this reconquest.

Justinian's true glory lay in his simplification and codification of the whole body of Roman law under four headings: the Institutes, the Code, the Digest and the Novels, the latter being recent laws. The other monument of his reign was the basilica of Saint Sophia in Constantinople, a real jewel of Byzantine art, with its huge dome, and the gold and marble of its interior decoration. We are also indebted to the Byzantine architects of the church of San Vitale at Ravenna.

Justinian's efforts of reconquest were to be without any future effects. Byzance came under the pressures of the Persians and the new enemies, the Slavs. In Italy, the Lombards founded a kingdom. Venice, which remained Byzantine, was to maintain its contact with the East.

The militant faith of the Christians of this era found expression in the monasteries which were being built in Barbarian Europe. In 529, Saint Benedict founded a monastery at Monte Cassino, in which he organised the strict Benedictine code of poverty and humility which his monks were to spread abroad. It was a Benedictine, Pope Gregory the Great (590—604 AD), who was to make the spiritual conquest of the Western Germanic Empire. The most extraordinary accomplishment of the first mediaeval Pope was the conversion of England. The Anglo-Saxon monasteries increased in number on the continent in the sixth and seventh centuries.

In the Far East, Buddhism spread throughout China and Japan. At the end of the year 618 AD, the T'ang dynasty gave China considerable power and a huge Empire which stretched from Korea to the Caspian Sea. But China became troubled. At one time the forces of wars and tyrannical power predominated; at another came revolution under a great leader who rallied the country together—until once again it became divided.

The Emperor T'ai-tsong (621—649 AD), was the man who brought about

The Schism of 1054

☐ **Catholics**
☐ **Greeks and Orthodox**

The Normans landing in England

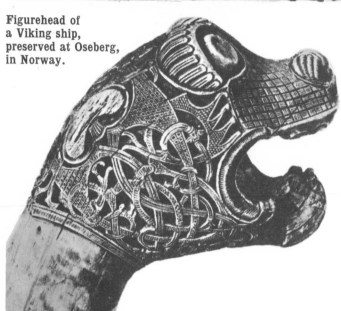

Figurehead of
a Viking ship,
preserved at Oseberg,
in Norway.

In a museum at Bayeux, a small town in Normandy, is the famous embroidery called the tapestry of Queen Matilda. Dating from the 11th century it is a strip of linen, 230 feet long and 20 inches wide, embroidered in wool. With an extraordinary vividness of colours and patterns, it retraces the episodes of the Norman conquest of England, including the Battle of Hastings.

ABOVE: The Norman army, seven thousand infantry and two thousand cavalry, land at Pevensey.

BELOW: King Edward the Confessor, whom the unfortunate Harold succeeded in 1066; Harold was himself killed that same year on the battle-field.

RIGHT: Their tools resting on their shoulders, the peasants come before their lord to find out the amount of their taxes. About 1,000 AD, European economy was founded on agriculture; trade was practically non-existent and craftsmen were few. Each feudal village, grouped around the lord's castle, constituted a tiny independent world, sufficient in itself. The peasants gave to the lord a proportion of their produce and a determined number of working days each year.

ABOVE: King Canute places a cross on an altar, helped by his wife, the queen. This ancient miniature wished to extol this king who ruled concurrently over England, Norway and Denmark, his military strength backed by Christian courage.

RIGHT: The basilica of Saint Mary Magdalene at Vézelay, one of the most beautiful of the Cluniac churches, where the barrel vault appeared for the first time in France

LEFT:
William
the Conqueror

Tournament between knights

Gregory VII
and Henry IV

Godfrey
de Bouillon

Crusaders' ship

Inca warrior

unity and power. He was not content only with military conquests. He restored the system of examinations for recruiting the most suitable officials. He took the lands away from the usurpers and redistributed them among the peasants. He began a system of taxation, and he favoured the craftsmen.

This was the era when the Chinese became masters in the art of manufacturing fine porcelain. Finally, the Emperor practised religious tolerance, not only in respect of the Buddhists, but also for the Christians who had come from Persia to spread their religion. In 638 AD, they were authorised to build the first Christian church in China.

About the year 600 AD, in a land which neither the West nor the Far East even suspected existed, Mexico, the Empire of the Mayas flourished. They are known to have had pyramids, a system of numerals and hieroglyphic writing, and a form of calendar.

Five years after Justinian's death, in 570 AD, Mohammed was born in a vast desert country—Arabia. Mohammed was a merchant who had travelled with the caravans of the Bedouin nomads who were in contact with the Oriental world. He understood that Arabia needed someone to channel its many tribes into a cohesive nation. He studied his surroundings and his times well and, in 610, at the age of 40, he announced that he was " the greatest and the last of the prophets ". He preached submission to one God, Allah, the creator of the universe.

Mohammed ran into trouble with pagans in Mecca and, in 622 AD, he fled to Medina, known as the city of the Prophet. This was the *Hegira*, the year one in the Mohammedan calendar. The great principles of the new religion of Islam were to be recorded by his disciples in the Koran.

On the death of Mohammed in 632 AD, his successors, the Caliphs Abu Bakr, Omar, Othman and Ali declared the ' Holy War ' to spread the teaching of the Prophet. In thirty years Islam was to triumph over all the Persian Empire and two-thirds of the Byzantine Empire, which was split by heresy.

The most prosperous Mohammedan kingdom was that of Syria where the Ommayads made Damascus their capital. Under the Ommayad Caliphate, the Arabs undertook new conquests after 660 AD, which led them into the Orient as far as Turkestan, India and even China. In the West they moved from Morocco across Spain to destroy the kingdom of the Visigoths in 711 AD. Nine years later they penetrated the Frankish kingdom. In 732 AD,

Saint Bernard preaching

at Poitiers, they found themselves opposing Charles Martel; this was the beginning of defeat for them.

In the Orient, in 678 AD, there was another check given to Arab expansion, in front of Constantinople.

The Arab Empire was much too vast and so it was divided up. In 750 AD, the Ommayads were to lose their power in Syria to the Abbasids (aided by the Persians) who moved the capital to Baghdad. One member of the Ommayads escaped and became ruler of the Moors as Abdul Rahman, Emir of Cordoba, which declared itself independent almost two hundred years later.

In Baghdad, the Caliph of the *Thousand and One Nights*, Harun Al-Rashid, (786—809 AD), gathered around him a court of rare magnificence and luxury, with poets, doctors, grammarians, musicians and artists.

In the course of one of their raids, in 751 AD, the Arabs formed an alliance with Turkestan against the Chinese. The Turks later became Mohammedans.

Despite local conflicts, China in the eighth century saw the peak of the T'ang dynasty, with the Emperor Hiuan-tsong. In his court the poets Li Po and Tu Fu sang of the pleasures and delights of life.

At the end of the century came the return of feudalism and eventually decay.

In Japan, great numbers of Buddhist monasteries were built. In 794 AD, Kyoto was founded and it remained the capital until the nineteenth century. The city was also known as Miyako meaning 'imperial city', and Heiankyo which meant 'capital of peace and tranquility'

In the kingdom of the Franks, Charles Martel, who had been victorious over the Arabs at Poitiers, was one of the mayors of the palace who managed to govern effectively under the failing power of the idle kings. His son, Pepin the Short, deposed the last Merovingian and took the title of king in 751 AD, with the support of Pope Zachary.

In return he helped the Pope against the Lombards whom he defeated in northern Italy. Pepin then gave the region situated around Rome to the Papacy. Thus the Pontifical States were created.

Pepin's son, Charlemagne, continued to support the Pope against the Lombards and he became king of Italy. He then conquered Germania after a difficult campaign against the Saxons. Charlemagne attempted to conquer Mohammedan Spain, but succeeded only in snatching Catalonia from the Arabs. During one of these expeditions Roland, Count of Brittany, was

Frederick Barbarossa

Monument to Henry the Lion
in Brunswick

Gothic window

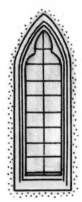

Minstrel

ABOVE: One of the best preserved fortresses erected by the Crusaders in Syria. Situated in an important strategic position and powerfully fortified, the stronghold was self-sufficient, containing wells, shops and living quarters.

BELOW: The duel between two famous heroes of the Crusades: Richard Coeur de Lion and Saladin. This picture is taken from an illustrated manuscript of that period. Note how the artist represented the Saracen as being evil.

Vertical lines and semicircular arches, light structures and flying buttresses, rose and stained-glass windows are the most characteristic features of Gothic architecture.

RIGHT AND LEFT: Stained-glass windows from the Cathedral at Chartres. One hundred and seventy stained windows and ten thousand statues of all types and sizes reflect the traditions, hopes and beliefs of the people of the twelfth and thirteenth centuries.

The camp of Genghis Khan

Saint Francis of Assisi

The Magna Carta

Frederick II

Castel del Monte

slaughtered at Roncevalles. This was the origin of the most beautiful *Chansons de Geste*, or epic poems, of the Middle Ages.

In the year 800 AD, Charlemagne had conquered all of Christian Europe, with the exception of Great Britain. The Pope crowned him Emperor. Thus the Roman Empire was restored and Charlemagne became the official supporter of the Catholic Church.

He then organised his Empire, dividing it into counties and establishing the *marches* to protect the frontiers. He had control over the Counts and Bishops by means of the *Missi dominici*, members of his entourage who twice a year followed a circuit, listening to cases and reporting back to the Emperor. These ambassadors took the laws, which were grouped under separate headings or chapters, to all the territories of the Empire.

But, despite these measures, provincialism became more marked, vassals were becoming semi-independent rulers, bishops were achieving positions of power and independence, and the stage was being set for the chaos that would follow Charlemagne's death.

One of Charlemagne's most important achievements was the foundation of schools close to the bishoprics. The Emperor even had one in his palace at Aachen, which had become his capital.

A new and very much more readable form of script called uncial writing appeared, used by the monks to copy out the Roman books. The monasteries became important centres of culture. The Emperor Charles was helped in literary matters by the scholars from his court: Alcuin of York, Paul Diacre of Lombard and his German biographer, Einhard.

After Louis the Pious (814—840 AD) a struggle for the succession began which had considerable consequences in Europe. Lothair, the eldest son of Louis, wanted to be the sole Emperor. His brothers, Louis and Charles, joined forces against him and in 842 they both took the Oath of Strasbourg. The text of the Oath was not written in Latin but in two other languages, Old German and Old French. In 843, Lothair was obliged to sign the Treaty of Verdun with his brothers. This divided up the great empire Charlemagne had created.

Charles the Bald received Western France; Louis the German acquired Eastern France, and Lothair got the Middle Kingdom, including Aachen, Lyons and Northern Italy.

This was the beginning of the European States system. On each side there

A monk at study

were territories which would gradually be formed into nations, and in the centre a corridor which would be the subject of much controversy.

After the death of Lothair, his kingdom was broken up. The Carolingians were unable to repel the attacks of the Norsemen who were overrunning Europe. The first invaders were the Magyar horsemen, who attacked the Slavonic peoples living in unorganised groups in the immense territory between the Baltic and the Balkans. These Magyars went as far as the Black Sea and then turned to Northern Italy.

The Vikings, or Norsemen, sailed along the Western coasts of Europe in their long warships and attacked with pre-planned precision. They landed with their horses and pillaged towns and villages, leaving so quickly that any retaliation was impossible. In this manner they attacked London, Nantes and Hamburg, setting up bases in Ireland and finally establishing veritable colonies on the coasts. King Alfred the Great (871—900 AD) divided the northern part of England among them on condition that their attacks should cease.

The Carolingian Empire suffered most from the attacks. In 885 AD, the Norsemen organised an expedition against Paris, which failed because of the organised defences led by Odo, Count of Paris. Dukes and Counts had to defend their own territories themselves, demonstrating the negligence of imperial power.

When the Emperor Charles the Fat was deposed, in 887 AD, Count Odo was proclaimed King of France. His descendants would be the Capetian kings. A conflict with the Carolingian Charles the Simple followed, during which Charles recognised Rollo the Dane as the first Duke of Normandy, where he had settled.

In Germany, the Hungarian raids overcame the last of the Carolingians. The Duke of Saxony, Henry the Fowler, founded the Saxon dynasty in 919. His son, Otto I, 936—973 AD, put an end to the revolts of the feudal lords, and in 955 achieved a decisive victory over the Hungarians. These latter then established a kingdom on the plain of the Danube, becoming Christians, with Saint Stephen as their king.

Otto I then pushed back the Slavs as far as the river Oder and, in 962 AD, the Pope crowned him Emperor of Rome.

His son, Otto II, had to halt the march to the East and bring back the frontier of the Empire to the Elbe.

In the kingdom of the Franks, henceforth called France, Hugh Capet was recognised as king owing to the actions of the bishops. His kingdom stretched from the Aisne to the Loire.

The Gotthard pass

Hanseatic city

Frederick II defeating the Mongols

Mounted highwayman

Itinerary of the voyages of Marco Polo. RIGHT: **A miniature of Genghis Khan, taken from a history of the Mongols by the Persian, Raschid ed-Din, 1596 AD**

Mongol building at Samarkand

Kublai Khan who received Marco Polo at his court

RIGHT: **Lübeck, on the Baltic Sea, ancient capital of the Hanseatic League. The League, a commercial confederation of free towns, grouped together the major ports between the Zuiderzee and the Gulf of Finland.**

OPPOSITE: **Saint Francis receives the Pope's approval for the founding of an order of Brothers. From a fresco in the Upper Basilica at Assisi. This is the work of Giotto, a great Italian painter of the 14th century.**

Marco Polo in China

A 13th century compass

Rudolph of Hapsburg

Dante Alighieri

The Oath on the Rütli Meadow

The efforts of the first Capetians were to assure their heredity, although they were opposed by Burgundy, Normandy, Brittany, Anjou and Aquitaine, which had their own sovereigns.

In the tenth century, the people of Europe lived in daily anxiety and were prey to a superstitious terror of the year 1,000. Though opposed by the feudal lords, the monasteries were to be the true centres of rejuvenation. The Abbey of Cluny, in Burgundy, founded in 910 AD by the Duke of Aquitaine, took upon itself the overwhelming task of re-establishing order in Christianity. The Abbots of Cluny first set to work to bring back to the clergy the meaning of their mission; to accomplish this, the abbots fought against Simony and opposed the marriage of priests. Then, against brutal feudal customs and ultimately against wars, they instituted the concepts of ' Peace of God ', later the ' Truce of God ' which limited fighting to certain days of the week and protected certain public buildings. They also attempted to instil in the nobility the spirit of chivalry and service.

About this time in China the Sung dynasty restored the centuries-old traditions in art and religion. The Chinese had invented a printing press with movable characters five centuries before Gutenberg. In Japan a feudal system began, and in Cambodia the Khymer Empire was nearing its peak, marked in the twelfth century by the building of the beautiful temples of Angkor. The Byzantine Empire saw a new awakening under Basil. He crushed the Bulgars of the Tsar Samuel in 1044 and achieved success over the Arabs and Turks. Under his influence, Vladimir, the Prince of Kiev, opened his doors to the clergy, thus giving birth to the Russo-Byzantine culture.

The Arab world, in spite of its divisions, was at the height of its civilisation. The mosques of Damascus and Cordoba are deservedly famous.

In Iran, among the Sassanids, lived the most famous representatives of the Islamic culture, formed from its Greek heritage and the contact with the Hindus. Such men as Avicenna, the doctor and philosopher who wrote the renowned *Canon of Medicine*, translated in the twelfth century, and read in most European universities; the Persian poet, Firdausi, and the mathematician, Al-Khowarizmi. The Hindu method of numbering, under the name 'Arabic numerals', has since been passed on to the West.

Other Moslems were also responsible for the glory of Islam at that time; the Turks who had taken possession of Northern India seized the emirate of Baghdad in 1055 AD. The tribes from Northern Africa journeyed into Spain, where the emirate of Cordoba was in decline.

The town of Marienburg

The discovery of gunpowder

On the mainland of Europe, the Norsemen continued their conquests. The Norwegian, Leif Ericson, colonised Greenland and landed at Labrador.

In 1016 AD, King Canute briefly unified England, Norway and Denmark into one kingdom. The bold Norsemen had now settled in France and were known as Normans. Some took possession of Southern Italy and others stayed North with William the Conqueror.

The Anglo-Saxon king, Edward the Confessor, had died without a son, and William, Duke of Normandy, claimed succession to the throne. He crossed the Channel with his army and met the Anglo-Saxons, with Harold as their leader.

A single victory at Hastings gave England to William. He was crowned king and, bringing over his knights and barons, he settled in England. The *Domesday Book* recorded the allocation of land.

William, King of England and Duke of Normandy, was paradoxically still a vassal of the king of France. Queen Matilda and her maids embroidered the Bayeux tapestry telling of the famous conquest.

The sovereigns of many European countries were coming into conflict with the Papacy. With the influence of the monks of Cluny behind them, the Popes wished to recover their temporal and spiritual independence. In 1059, Pope Nicholas decreed that the sovereign pontiff would be elected by the cardinals. In 1074, Hildebrand, a monk from Cluny, became Pope Gregory VII and forbade the election of bishops by the laity. This was the decisive step that set in motion the quarrel with the Empire.

In 1076, Emperor Henry IV deposed the Pope, who in turn excommunicated Henry. Troubles and civil war incited Henry to ask the Pope's pardon, at Canossa. But soon the struggle began again, and in 1084 it was Gregory VII who had to take the road of exile.

In 1122, the Concordat of Worms put an end to the quarrel, with a compromise thought of by a French cleric: the bishops were to be elected by the clergy but they would receive their temporal powers from the sovereigns or lords. Meanwhile, the Church of Rome had become separated from that of Constantinople.

Europe in the eleventh century had increased in population, and her prosperity had grown with her technical progress. The lands ravaged by invasions and local quarrels were cleared and cultivated. The harness was invented, making it possible for horses to plough the earth. Water mills increased in number. The monks built beautiful Roman churches.

Teutonic knight

Procession to ward off the Black Death

The seven elector princes

Portrait of Francis Petrarch, Italian poet and scholar, whose sonnets to a woman called Laura established him as one of the greatest love poets. His poems could be considered as the first modern work of Italian literature.

OPPOSITE PAGE: The Palace of the Popes at Avignon. Constructed in the 14th century, it was the seat of the pontiffs during a period called the 'Babylonian captivity'. This period of captivity lasted from 1305 to 1377 when, yielding to the insistence and persuasion of St. Catherine of Siena, Pope Gregory XI returned to Rome.

ABOVE: Print of a manuscript from a famous library in Milan, which illustrates an episode from Dante's *Divine Comedy*. Dante and Virgil are in Hell, guarded by the centaur, Cacus, who is ridden by a dragon which throws out flames at those he meets.

RIGHT: Monument of William Tell, erected in Altdorf, chief town of the canton of Uri, where the legendary hero was supposed to have begun the struggle for Helvetian independence at the beginning of the 14th century.

Port of a Hanseatic city

Mediaeval dress

John Huss

Joan of Arc

Renaissance window

All this energy in Europe found an outlet in the Crusades.

Since the tenth century the places of pilgrimage in the East had increased in number. A century later the Christian kingdoms in Spain set about the reconquest of the Moslems. The spirit of these battles is illustrated in the exploits of Rodrigo Diaz, The Cid.

In 1085, Alphonse VII, the king of Castile, took Toledo. The Spanish Moslems then called to their aid the North African Berbers, a tribe of strict faith. French knights began to journey to the Spanish coasts to fight the infidels. In the East, the Seljuk Turks overran Asia Minor, taking it from the Byzantines; then, already masters of the caliphate of Baghdad, they seized Jerusalem in 1078. Byzantium begged for help.

In 1095, at the Synod of Clermont, Pope Urban II made his celebrated appeal, mainly to France, for a crusade . . . " People of France, a race beloved of God . . . the country you live in is too confined for your large population. Put an end to your disputes. Take the road to the Holy Sepulchre and snatch the country from the foul hands of the Turks . . . Do this in remission for your sins."

Immediately, amidst cries of " It's God's will ", and with a red cross on their shoulders, the pilgrims set off in a great throng across Germany, Hungary and Bulgaria. The first crusade, in 1096, known as the Peasants' Crusade, which consisted of thousands of poor men following the monk, Peter the Hermit, was wiped out by the Turks in Asia Minor. Later, armies of French, German and Flemish knights set out for the Holy Land with their respective leaders.

In 1099, Jerusalem was captured and Godfrey de Bouillon became king, with his brother Baldwin as heir. On their journey to the Holy Land the other knights had established French States at Antioch, Edessa and Tripoli. The formation of these states instigated a great stream of change in the West, which led to the prosperity of the Italian ports of Genoa and Venice.

The Byzantine Empire gained nothing from the Crusades, for the Crusaders were just as eager to seize the Byzantine territories as the Turks had been.

During the next 200 years there were more Crusades. To protect the Christian States, orders such as the Knights Templar, Knights Hospitaller and Teutonic Knights were formed. The latter later transferred their efforts to the Baltic shores.

France, who had furnished the largest contingents of Crusaders, now began

Printing works   **Gutenberg**

The Doge of Venice

A condottiere

Florentine merchant

to assume a new importance in Europe. After the influence of Cluny came that of Cîteaux. The Cistercians sought to revive an appreciation of the true Christian values. They themselves devoted their lives to working in the fields. The first Abbot of the monastery at Clairvaux was St. Bernard, whose zeal spread even to the kings and Popes.

St. Bernard preached very fervently for the Second Crusade, and he also condemned the philosophy of Peter Abelard, whose theological conceptions he judged to be heretical.

King Louis VI of France, counselled by Abbot Suger of St. Denys, extended the royal authority. He married his son to Eleanor, the heir to the Duchy of Aquitaine. But, after the death of Suger, the couple were divorced and Eleanor married Henry of Anjou, who two years later, in 1154, became Duke of Normandy and King of England.

Thus the Capetian domain in France was menaced by defeat from a king who ruled a kingdom which stretched from Scotland to the Pyrénées. But Henry II's reign was increasingly taken up with quarrels with the Church. Finally, he ordered the assassination of the Archbishop of Canterbury, his friend Thomas Beckett, who opposed him. This caused a great scandal and the king had to make public repentance on the tomb of the archbishop.

In the Holy Roman Empire, Frederick Barbarossa, 1152—1190 AD, wanted to re-establish German domination of Italy. He destroyed Milan and other cities but was finally overcome by the Lombard League. Meanwhile, by the marriage of his son to Constance of Sicily, the Empire took root in Southern Italy.

In the East, the French states became again involved in war with the Turks. In 1187, Sultan Saladin seized Jerusalem, after conquering Syria and Egypt. All the European sovereigns set out for the Holy Land: Philip Augustus of France, Richard the Lionheart of England and Frederick Barbarossa, who died, by drowning, in Asia Minor. The Crusaders succeeded only in capturing Acre, which became the capital of the French Empire in the East, up to its fall in 1291.

The Fourth Crusade, organised by Pope Innocent III in an attempt to give new force to the Church, was diverted from its target by the Venetians, who persuaded the Crusaders to sack Constantinople. Villehandouin, who took part in this encounter, related the story of the taking of the town in 1204 in his *Chronicles* and also the installation of the Latin Empire of Constantinople. The Byzantine Empire was restored in 1261 AD.

Birth-place of
Joan of Arc
at Domrémy, France

BELOW, LEFT: **Detail from** *The Expulsion of Adam and Eve from the Garden of Eden,* **a painting by Masaccio which hangs in the Brancacci chapel in Florence. Masaccio was the initiator and principal artisan of Renaissance painting. Although he died young, he dominated his century by his exceptional personality. In the Nordic countries, the influence of the Renaissance led to a great realism, as is shown in this painting by Cranach** (BELOW, RIGHT), **in which the Elector of Saxony is treated with a merciless candour.**

The facade of the Strozzi Palace, in Florence. Work of the architect Benedetto da Majano, this is a typical example of Italian Renaissance architecture with the regularly spaced windows which give an impression of classical harmony.

The cupola of the Cathedral of Santa Maria del Fiore, work of Filippo Brunelleschi. When Brunelleschi began to build in the new method, this innovation went unnoticed. In fact, there had been no real, great change in style since the Renaissance in Italy drew its inspiration from the ancient classical traditions, which had never died out in this country.

The Palace of the Doges, in Venice, looking onto the canal. The Renaissance gave Venice a singular aspect which drew its inspiration both from Gothic art and from the particular situation of this town.

The taking of Constantinople

The voyage of Bartholomew Diaz

Alhambra, ancient palace and fortress at Granada

Christopher Columbus

Christopher Columbus at San Salvador

Another enterprise of Pope Innocent III had more success. In 1212, he formed a coalition to support the kingdoms of Aragon and Castile in their struggles against the Arabs. After the battle of Las Navas de Tolosa their success continued and soon the Arabs were left only with Granada, which was finally taken from them by the Catholic kings in 1492.

Finally Innocent III sent the Spaniard St. Dominic and his friars against the heretics known as Catharists, in the South of France, after their murder of the Papal Legate. The barons from the North of France were invited to join the Crusade. Led by Simon de Montfort, they wiped out the Albigensians in 1223. The Inquisition was established in 1229 to reinforce the effects of the Crusade.

In 1249, Toulouse was annexed by France. Philip Augustus, taking advantage of the death of Richard the Lionheart, seized Normandy, Poitou, Anjou, the Maine and Touraine from King John of England. John made an alliance with Emperor Otto IV against Philip Augustus. The coalition was defeated by Philip at Bouvines in 1214. The French royalty came away from the victory with great triumph. On the other hand the English barons took advantage of John's defeat by forcing him to accept the Magna Carta, which limited the royal power.

Philip Augustus now began to modify the structure of his kingdom. The king was represented in the provinces by the magistrates and seneschals, who administered justice. The towns which were developing with the progress of trade and craftsmen freed themselves from external control, their rights being fixed in their charters. The formation of these communities contributed to the reinforcement of the bourgeoisie or middle classes, who supported the monarchs against the lords.

In Paris, which had become the capital of France, the first mediaeval university enjoyed great fame. Sorbon, chaplain to Louis IX, founded the college of Sorbonne, where St. Thomas Aquinas taught at the end of the thirteenth century.

Gothic architecture had now superseded the Roman style. The architecture of churches became much more airy because of the use of ribbed vaultings and flying buttresses. The Cathedrals in the cities became great masterpieces.

The songs of the wandering troubadors and the Arthurian verse of Chrétien de Lesges was succeeded by the bourgeois literature of Jean de Meung and the satirical legends of Reynard the Fox, with their acid comments on the nobility and clergy from the peasants' point of view.

From 1229 to 1270, Louis IX reigned in France. Also known as Saint Louis,

Albrecht Dürer in his attic

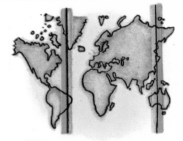

☐ **Portugal**
☐ **Spain**

Vasco da Gama

Girolamo Savonarola

Aztec deity

he typified the ideal of the Mediaeval Christian sovereign. His sense of justice expressed itself in the creation of such institutions as the High Judicial Court in Paris, and the development of the right of appeal. He attempted to settle the quarrels of the kingdom by negotiation. The Treaty of Paris, signed with England in 1259, gave back Normandy, Anjou, Maine, Touraine and Poitu in exchange for the Duchy of Guyenne and the recognition of Henry III as Duke of Aquitaine.
Louis' piety urged him to join the last Crusades. His first attempt ended in Egypt and his second journey in Tunis, where he died of the plague in 1270 AD.

With Frederick II, the Empire once again came into conflict with the Papacy. The Emperor had his residence, inherited from his mother, in Sicily. He was of sceptical faith and probably atheistic. He lived, as did later the princes of the Renaissance, surrounded by Arab, Christian and Jewish scholars and philosophers.
The Popes, Gregory IX and Innocent IV, incited all Catholic Europe against him. After his death the Kingdom of the Two Sicilies was detached from the Empire and went to the brother of Louis IX, Charles d'Anjou. The Empire suffered an interregnum of twenty years.

Asia in the thirteenth century saw the appearance of Genghis Khan. In twenty years (1206—1227) this Mongol chieftain took Pekin and Northern China, and sent his horsemen on terrifying raids as far as Afghanistan and the Ukraine. At his death his kingdom stretched from the China Sea to the Volga. In 1280, Kublai Khan, a grandson of Genghis, proclaimed himself Emperor of China. Thus he became the master of one of the oldest and most highly developed civilisations in the world.
A Venetian named Marco Polo set out on a voyage to trade with this marvellous civilisation. When he returned he told of all the sights he had seen—theatres, restaurants, lakes with boats full of musicians, and women, whom he said " looked just like fairies "
This was the period when the middle classes in Europe began to think about politics. In England, in 1265, they had obtained the right to be consulted along with the barons by the king about the country's expenditure. This was quite just, as they paid a lot of taxes themselves, but they took advantage of their meetings to speak of other political matters. The house where they met came to be called Parliament.

ABOVE, LEFT: **Self-portrait of Albrecht Dürer.** RIGHT: **The Turkish fortress of Rumeli Hisar on the Bosphorus. It is said that a thousand masons were engaged in its construction, which was ordered by Mehmet II, in 1452, in readiness for the siege of Byzantium.**

OPPOSITE PAGE: **French miniature portraying the capture of Byzantium**

LEFT: **Pyramid at Tula, Mexico. Before the Aztecs, the Toltecs reigned in Mexico for 500 years, until the 13th century. Their capital was Tula, where we can still admire the majestic temples in the form of pyramids, dedicated to the Sun and to the Moon.**

ABOVE: **Detail from one of the statuettes which adorn the pyramid.**

Messenger   Patrician   Maidservant

Italian costumes of 16th century

Leonardo da Vinci

Copernicus

Peter Henlein's watch

Castle on the banks of
the River Loire

In the Swiss Alps, other middle classes and mountain folk refused to pay their feudal dues to Rudolph of Hapsburg. They revolted and fought against him. They were excellent soldiers, and the legend goes that one of them, William Tell, was able to pierce an apple placed on his son's head with a cross-bow bolt. Their revolt gave birth to the first Swiss cantons.

In France King Philip IV, called Philip the Fair, 1285—1314 AD, came into conflict with the Pope. He opposed on principle the world domination of the Church and aimed resolutely for an absolute, national monarchy. He created a sort of parliament known as the States-General, where the nobles, bourgeoisie and clergy were represented.
Pope Boniface was arrested by Philip at Anagni and later died in captivity. His successor, Clement V, transferred the Papal residence to Avignon. This was the prelude to the Great Schism, which was caused by the existence of two Popes, one in Rome and the other at Avignon.
The State created by Philip IV soon met with troubles. His three sons having died without heirs, the throne was claimed by the King of England, Edward III, who had married Philip's daughter. But in France monarchs' daughters were not allowed to rule. Edward declared war in 1337 and this war lasted 100 years. In a Europe deeply troubled by famine and epidemics—a third of the population was wiped out by the Black Death—this war led to important changes, including the use of gunpowder and the invention of the first ordnance.

In Italy, constant scene of the struggles between the papacy and the Holy Roman Empire, the Florentine Dante (1265—1321), one of the greatest poets that ever lived, wrote the *Divine Comedy*, not in Latin, as was customary, but in Tuscan, the language spoken by the people.
On the other side of Europe, Russia, which was still no more than a grand-duchy, made Moscow its capital. On the other side of the ocean, in America, a continent which was to remain unknown to the Europeans until the following century, the Aztecs built their capital, Tenochtitlan, which was situated north of Mexico.
Europe had not recovered from the Black Death which, moreover, was to reappear from time to time until the middle of the 15th century.
In Germany, the Hanseatic League, a commercial association consisting of approximately 160 towns, was established. It opened the doors of trade to Stockholm, Berger and London. This league lost its power as the nations

Magellan explained his plans at the Spanish court

Jacob Fugger

of Europe became stronger.

Lithuania, having become Christian through the marriage of Queen Edwige to the prince of Lithuania, Ladislaus II, allied itself with Hungary and Poland in order to put a curb on the Germanic power.

Denmark, Sweden and Norway united themselves into a single state whilst, in France, the duchy of Burgundy, to which also belonged the Netherlands, Flanders and Brabant, became a cultural and commercial centre of great wealth.

In 1418 the Council of Constance put an end to the Great Schism by electing a single Pope, Martin V, who was to reside, once more, at Rome.

The doctrine of Luther

The Hundred Years' War continued and France was at its lowest. A young peasant girl from Lorraine, Joan of Arc, presented herself to the king of France, Charles VII, at Chinon, where he had taken refuge from the English who occupied almost the whole country. She told him that she had heard voices which urged her to deliver France.

The king, impressed by her zeal and courage, put her at the head of a small army. She compelled the English to lift the siege of Orléans and safely conveyed Charles VII to Rheims for his coronation.

Wounded, betrayed and taken prisoner, Joan was afterwards declared a heretic by the English and burnt at the stake in the market place at Rouen on 30 May, 1431.

The Turks in Egypt

In spite of all these wars and the after-effects of the plague, the world was ready for change in all its forms: cultural, artistic, scientific. In England, the modern Gothic style of architecture was born, which was to be found again in the Houses of Parliament in 1840. In France, the flamboyant style appeared, notably in the cathedral of Amiens. The middle classes built comfortable, easy-to-heat houses.

Cortes conquered Mexico

In Italy, humanism was born. This movement held that man is the source of all activity, discovery, production and knowledge, and it sought the expansion of all human qualities. Painters and sculptors of genius, such as Donatello, Fra Angelico, Verrocchio, Piero della Francesca, Botticelli, and many others showed the people of this era that the world was populated by admirable and impressive figures, whether their greatness lay in their youth, their fame or

The celebrated *Mona Lisa* by Leonardo da Vinci. Da Vinci was a very personal painter and he developed a technique in which he obtained completely original effects by his clever use of shades, so that the finished painting, with its effect of half-lights, seemed to be enveloped in mystery. But Leonardo da Vinci was not just a painter; he was the most versatile genius of his time, who interested himself in all aspects of science and engineering. Among his many works are found an imaginary mechanism to turn back an enemy's attack (ILLUSTRATED BELOW) and a study of flight (ILLUSTRATED BELOW, LEFT). The horseman was a sketch for the monument of Francesco Sforza. Although the full-scale model for this statue was completed, it was never cast and was destroyed by invading French soldiers, 1499.

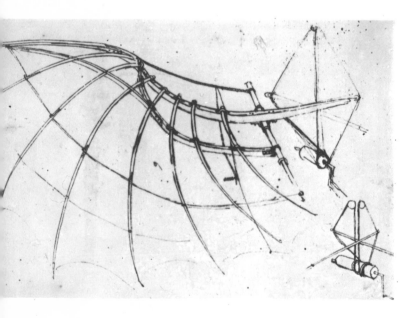

In the fifteenth and sixteenth centuries the costumes of the nobles were enriched, thanks to the refinements of fashion and the variety of materials: silks, damasks, brocades and velvets. Even the costumes of the soldiers were very elegant with richly coloured cloaks, which gave protection against the wind, and fine embroidery. The ordinary people continued to dress themselves in garments made of wool and hemp, as in the past (ILLUSTRATION, TOP RIGHT). BOTTOM, RIGHT: A lady in a robe and train, depicted in a 15th century painting.

BELOW: Louis XII, King of France, leads his army to march against Italy. Prudent and calculating, the successor of Charles VIII launched into the Italian Wars and, in his capacity as heir to Valentine Visconti, he put forward his claims to Milan, which he conquered without difficulty (1949-1500).

Sultan Solomon II

An iconoclast, or breaker of images

Gustavus I of Sweden

A turkey-cock of South America

Luther at the Diet of Worms

their beauty. The poets Boccaccio and Petrarch also extolled the new spirit. The German printer, Gutenberg, discovered printing with movable type, an invention which enabled the increase of works which, until then, had only existed as manuscripts in convent libraries.

During this time, sailors embarked upon great voyages in the Atlantic Ocean. The Portuguese tried to reach the Indies by going round Africa in their ships of the high seas, the 'caravels', which from that time were provided with compasses, helms, and armed with cannons. In 1487, they reached the Cape of Good Hope. In 1498, Vasco da Gama rounded Africa and thus opened a route to the Indies. The voyages greatly enriched the Portuguese, for Africa supplied them with gold and spices, and Lisbon flourished.

In 1492, the year of the downfall of Granada, the Genoese Christopher Columbus obtained from Queen Isabella of Spain the means to undertake the voyage which must, he thought, allow him to reach the Indies via the west. Days passed and still no land was sighted. The discouraged sailors wanted to turn back. But, on 12 October, the expedition discovered an island of the Bahamas which Christopher Columbus christened San Salvador. Convinced that he had disembarked at the Indies, he gave the name Indians to the natives who came to meet his sailors. In three successive voyages he was to discover the coast of Cuba, the mouth of the Orinoco, and central America, which he continued to believe was the Indies.

It was not until ten years later that it was realised that this was the discovery of a new world which was not Asia and which should have been called Columbia, but was, in fact, to bear the name of the Florentine explorer, Amerigo Vespucci.

In 1494, the Treaty of Tordesillas gave the discovered territories in America to Spain, and those in Africa and India to Portugal.

At this period, England had not yet become a contender in the field of exploration and the French were too occupied with fighting each other to trouble themselves with the discovery of other lands. In 1453, the French succeeded in driving the English from their country. England maintained only Calais. Charles VII, aided by his great Minister of Finance, Jacques Coeur, re-established his authority over the kingdom of France by creating a permanent army supplied with artillery.

Succeeding Charles, Louis XI, 1461—1483, undertook a fierce struggle against the greatest of his feudal lords, Charles the Bold, Duke of Burgundy,

Francisco Pizarro
at the conquest of Peru

The rising of the peasants

A lancer carrying
a lance of 16½ feet

The first vice

Charles V

and he succeeded in returning to the control of the crown, not only the duchy of Burgundy, but also Picardy, Anjou, Maine and Provence. In order to develop the economy he created the fairs of Lyon, where the merchants of Flanders, Germany and Italy met.

His son, Charles VIII, who was no more than a child when he succeeded to the throne in 1483, was soon to engage in somewhat senseless wars in Italy, in an attempt to conquer the northern part of that country. He succeeded only in bringing back the Renaissance to France.

England was no sooner finished with the Hundred Years' War than it was ravaged by the Wars of the Roses, a feud between two families who pretended to the throne: the House of Lancaster, who had for its emblem a red rose, and the House of York, whose emblem was the white rose. In 1485, at the Battle of Bosworth, Henry Tudor, of the House of Lancaster, defeated and killed King Richard III. Thirty years of spasmodic civil war was over. To strengthen his right to the throne, Henry Tudor married Elizabeth, the daughter of King Edward IV of York.

Henry was a particularly energetic king. England owed to him its commercial prosperity and the progress of the middle classes. He made himself the protector of small landowners, granting them the right to vote if they had a revenue of forty shillings. He had such a submissive Parliament that in the twenty-four years of his reign (1485—1509) they assembled only seven times.

The year 1453 not only marked the end of the Hundred Years War but also the end of the Byzantine Empire. Mohammed Ali took Constantinople, named it Istanbul, and it became peopled by Moslems, Slavs, Armenians, and then by the Jews who had fled from the persecutions of Queen Isabella and King Ferdinand in Spain. The cathedral of Saint Sophia, glory of the Eastern Orthodox Church, became a mosque.

It was under these conditions that Ivan III, 1462—1505, who put an end to the Mongolian domination and integrated the trading republic of Novgorod into the new Russian State, declared himself the successor to the emperors of the East. He married the daughter of the last of these emperors and took the title of Tsar, or Czar, that is to say Caesar.

Charles VIII, and then Louis XII, engaged in wars in Italy which served no

Francis I, painted by Jean Clouet. RIGHT, TOP TO BOTTOM:
Different types of armour used by soldiers of the 16th century;
armour was also provided for the dogs, as is shown here on
the dog of Charles V, exhibited at the Military Museum in
Madrid.

ON THE OPPOSITE PAGE: An impressive view of the ruins of
Machu Picchu in north-east Peru. A fortress of the Incas,
its altitude is 6,560 feet and it lies in the heart of a chain of
mountains between impassable summits.

Saint Ignatius Loyola and the Pope

Luther's bible

John Calvin

The medicine of Paracelsus

Henry VIII outside his palace at Hampton Court

purpose but to discover the marvels created by the Italians in the 15th century, known in Italy as the Quattrocento. The Renaissance was much more than a resurrection of the ancient world. It was a formidable explosion of life, and this was to show itself, in France, in the Loire Valley, where sumptuous royal residences were constructed, such as Blois, Chambord, Chenonceaux, Azay-le-Rideau, which housed masterpieces of Italian and French painting. Italian sculptors and painters like Cellini and Leonardo da Vinci came to stay in France. The poets Marot, du Bellay, Ronsard regained forgotten elegance. Even female poets such as Louise Labbe were born. The great humour of Rabelais expressed, in *Garguntua* and *Pantagruel*, the joy of life. However, there are three Italians who best represented the tendencies of the mood of the time: the baroque power of Michelangelo, the versatile genius of Leonardo da Vinci and the classical grace of Raphael.

Every country in Europe participated in the movement, each according to its temperament. In Flanders, the Bruegels and Jerome Bosch mingled realism and fantasy. In Germany, Dürer brought a cruel but admirable precision to drawing. And the Earth itself appeared in a new light: the Polish Copernicus discovered that it revolved around the sun.

There were also men, who were neither artists nor scientists, who made conquests which, although less aesthetic, were by no means less important. The conquest of Mexico by the Spaniard, Cortés, was an incredible adventure. This thirty-three-year-old captain landed in Mexico with 32 cross-bowmen, 13 arquebusiers, 110 sailors, 200 Indians, 10 cannons and 13 horses, and he conquered a kingdom larger than Spain, inhabited by ten million people.

The masters of this country were called the Aztecs; their leader was the emperor Montezuma II.

They were much more civilised than the other Indians, but they had never seen a horse. When they sighted the horsemen, they took them for mighty warriors who had two arms and four legs. They believed in the wicked gods and they lived in fear of the return of one of them whom they had driven away. At first they thought that Cortés was this god.

Cortés easily conquered the coast, and the Indians of this region, who endured with reluctance the absolute power of the emperor Montezuma, united themselves with him. Cortés had an army of 4,000 men when he arrived before the great city of Tenochtitlán, whose buildings rose up from the bed of the shallow Lake Texcoco. The emperor welcomed him as if he were a god, and accommodated him in his father's old palace. But when Cortés upturned the idols to which the Aztecs made human sacrifices, the Aztecs

The Council of Trent

Ivan the Terrible

rebelled and chased the Spaniards from the city. The latter returned in force and their guns and cannons brought down the capital of the Aztecs. Cortés found himself master of inexhaustible treasures, from which the king of Spain was to benefit (1521).

At the same time, Magellan's sailors made the first voyage around the world—Magellan himself died en route in the Philippines—and returned to Spain with a cargo of spices which brought nearly enough money to finance the voyage.

Several years previous, in 1513, Balboa had crossed the isthmus of Panama and discovered a vast sea, the Pacific Ocean. With him was an adventurer who could not even read, Francois Pizarro. Hearing the natives say that by navigating this sea towards the south, one arrived at a country where there were great quantities of gold, Pizarro dreamed of conquering this land.

Michelangelo

In 1542, he sailed from Panama with 114 men. But he failed three times before reaching the island of Gallo, off the coast of Ecuador. He went to Spain to inform the king, Charles V, of the fabulous riches which were to be found in this country called Peru. Charles granted him the governorship of the country, on condition that he captured it. In 1531, Pizarro landed in Peru with a small army.

The inhabitants were called Incas. They lived in a sort of socialist society, strictly subordinated by the supreme Inca who was, at the same time, a king, a priest and a god. He commanded an army of officials who were responsible for local administration.

They had a great sense of honour and it was this honour which was to cause their downfall. The Inca, Atahualpa, declared that he wished to be the friend of the strangers and presented himself, unarmed, at Pizarro's quarters; the body of an ambassador was sacred, to have come armed would have been a grave discourtesy. He was presented with a Bible in order that he might learn of the true God. The true God! He was the true god. He threw the Bible to the ground.

" Santiago! " cried Pizarro. It was the agreed signal, and a cannon fired in reply. The Spaniards massacred the retinue of Incas and Pizarro took Atahualpa prisoner.

This utilisation of Christ and his teachings for the satisfaction of greedy

The first tobacco plantation in Spain

Oranges from China

93

ON THE OPPOSITE PAGE: **Detail from the painting** *The Triumph of Death* **by Pieter Breughel, the Flemish painter. In this work the artist reveals the horrors of the religious wars which caused such havoc in Europe in the middle of the 16th century. Massacres and tortures, in a nightmarish atmosphere where human beings were reduced to the state of skeletons, demonstrated the destructive elements of human nature unleashed by war.**

LEFT, TOP TO BOTTOM: **Fragments from** *The Last Judgement* **by Michelangelo, which is in the Sistine Chapel in Rome; the resurrection of the dead, the resurrection of Christ, the damned. Michelangelo worked by himself for fifty-four years to paint the Sistine Chapel, stopping only to eat. These paintings have an impressive power and drama rarely attained.**

Thomas More, the English chancellor who, as he was a Catholic, opposed the Reformation and was condemned to death.

BELOW: **Anne Boleyn, second wife of Henry VIII and mother of Elizabeth I.**

Elizabeth I of England   **Akbar the Great**

Francis Drake

The Puritans

Admiral Coligny

instincts was a clear indication of the confusion of spirit then existing. It was this abuse which led a German monk, Martin Luther, to affix his ninety-five theses to a church door in Wittenburg on 31 October, 1517. Luther's writings attacked the trade of selling indulgences, which were sold even over the counters of the Fugger bank.

Luther believed that a Christian acquired the mercy of God not by his own acts, nor again by his money, but by virtue of his faith in God. He wanted Christian thought to return to the Bible and he contested the authority of the Pope. The Pope, in turn, ordered Luther to recant his doctrines and, when Luther refused, the Pope excommunicated him. Luther publicly tore up the Bull of Excommunication. Banned from the empire, he found refuge with Frederick of Saxony. His doctrine, called either Lutheranism or Protestantism, spread across Germany and was the cause of bitter wars between Protestants and Catholics.

The teachings of Luther were interpreted for the French nation by John Calvin at Geneva. Calvin taught that we are born polluted with the stain of sin and thus incapable of achieving our own salvation. Only God can save those whom He chooses, and only those who have faith in God and believe will be chosen. This form of Protestantism, called Calvinism, spread through France.

The Council of Trent, in order to unite the Catholic church in the face of the Protestant threat, restated the doctrines of the Catholic church and clearly defined its dogmas: the real presence of Christ in the Eucharist, the doctrine of Purgatory, the veneration of the saints and the spiritual authority of the Pope.

Church discipline was also defined: the use of Latin in church services, the celibacy of priests, the creation of seminaries for the training of religious, etc. Many abuses were banned at this reforming Council.

The firm of Fugger, the Pope's bankers who sold indulgences, financed and achieved the election of Charles V of Spain to the Imperial title in 1519, to succeed the Emperor Maximilian. Francis I of France, who was also a

Procession to the monastery

William Shakespeare

The arrest of Egmont

Potato plant

Venetian galley

candidate, was foolish enough to pay the electors in advance for the support they never gave him.

Charles V, Lord of Spain and Spanish America, of Sardinia, Sicily, Naples, the Netherlands, Flanders, Alsace, France-Comte, Artois, Austria, and of the German Hapsburg possessions, could truly say that the sun never set on his territories.
But to hold together these scattered states cost him much more than they yielded him. American money was not enough; he was always in debt to the bank of Fugger. This bank acquired such power that it has been said that she held in her grip the two halves of the world: the Pope and the Emperor.
All through his reign the poor but magnificent Charles V never ceased his battle against his three adversaries: France, the German Protestant princes and the Turks. The latter disputed his mastery of the Mediterranean and menaced his empire in central Europe; they advanced as far as Vienna in 1529, but were repulsed.
Francis I was not averse to making an alliance with the Turks against Charles V, to the great repugnance of the Christians and also of the Protestant princes.
After the death of Francis I, his son Henry II continued the struggle for power.

In 1556, a discouraged Charles V abdicated and retired to a monastery. He divided his empire: to his brother, Ferdinand I, he gave the imperial crown and the German territories; to his son, Philip II, he gave the Netherlands and Spain, his Italian possessions and his colonies.
The Peace of Augsburg, 1555, gave the German Protestant princes and their subjects freedom to practise their religion. The House of Hapsburg also acceded that each ruler should have the right to decide the religion of his state.

In 1559, Philip II concluded an inherited war against France by signing the Treaty of Cateau-Cambrésis with Henry II. Philip was penniless, despite his American treasures, and his creditors, the Fugger bank, made him bankrupt. France was not in much better straits.
Only England, under the long reign of Henry VIII, 1509—1547, had maintained a stability which presaged the great reign of Elizabeth I. To achieve this happy position Henry had practised a clever game of see-saw politics

ABOVE: A view of the royal chase, from a Mongol miniature. Mongol art flourished in India at the time of the great Mogul empire, founded by Baber, who claimed descent from the mongol conqueror, Genghis Khan, and consolidated by Akbar and his son, Jahan. The Mongol empire did not endure long: it proved easy for the English, at the end of the 18th century, to merge it, little by little, with India.

ABOVE: A fragment of a painting by Paolo Veronese, Italian painter, showing one of the many sea battles of that era.

Three-masted English vessel of the 16th century, furnished with a number of cannons on the lower deck. With a similar boat, Francis Drake fought the Spanish galleys.

ABOVE: **The School at Strat-ford-on-Avon, the native village of Shakespeare, the greatest English poet and dramatist.**

BELOW: **View of London at the time of Elizabeth I. One can see, along the Thames, the Globe theatre, where the Shakespearean dramas were played; on the other bank is the Blackfriars Theatre, reserved for a more intellectual public.**

The night of the Saint Bartholomew massacre

Duke of Alba

The Turks at Tunis

A teacher of the 16th century

Siberian trappers

between France and the Hapsburgs. He had also managed to preserve England from a religious war—such as were tearing Europe apart at this time—by his proclamation that the King was head of the Church in England, declared in the Acts of Supremacy of 1534 and in the Bill of Six Articles of 1539.

In France, the accidental death of Henry II in a tournament left the throne to his son, Francis II, an infant who only reigned for one year, then to Charles IX, who reigned for ten years. Their mother, Catherine de Medici, acted as regent. The country was divided between Catholics and Protestants and the massacre of some Protestants at Wassy in Champagne, in 1562, was the signal for the start of a religious war which lasted until 1598. The Catholics appealed to the Spaniards for help, while the Protestants enlisted the help of the Germans and the English. The great Catholic Guise family and the Protestant Bourbons—both of whom had ambitions to supplant the monarchy —were strengthened by the wars and by the frailty of the royal family. A very sad and infamous event took place during these years: the St. Bartholomew's Massacre, which was sanctioned by Catherine de Medici on 24 August, 1572.

Henry III, who succeeded his brother Charles IX in 1574, soon faced a revolt led by Henry of Guise, leader of the Catholic League, who was supported by Philip II.

It was clear that the Guise family were prepared to challenge Henry for the French throne. The Duke of Guise became so popular—he was nicknamed ' the King of Paris '—that Henry had him assassinated in 1588. Parisians, hearing the news, wept in the streets. They had lately mocked the king, but now the people's vengeance did not limit itself to mockery. In 1589, when Henry III presented himself outside his capital, the Catholic party sent a fanatical monk to stab him at Saint-Cloud.

His Protestant cousin, Henry of Navarre, succeeded to the throne of France. It took Henry seven years to become master of his own kingdom, with numerous battles against the Catholic League and the Spaniards. It was Henry who, as he plunged into the Battle of Ivry on 14 March, 1590, uttered the famous battle cry: '' Rally to my white standard and you will find the road to victory and honour.''

Henry put an end to the religious wars with the famous saying '' Paris is well

The Tower of London

The astronomer Tycho Brahé

worth a Mass ", when, in 1593, he took the decisive step of becoming a Catholic. Now Paris opened its doors to Henry. The religious wars were finally ended by Henry's publication of the Edict of Nantes in 1598; this allowed liberty of conscience and private worship to Protestants throughout France. It now fell upon Henry to save France from ruin, from the disasters of civil wars and the threat of Spanish occupation. He must win the confidence of the people, turning their hatred into affection, so that he might stabilise the economy and ' put a chicken on every dinner table in France '. By his cheerfulness and good sense he succeeded, with the aid of his friend and chief minister, the Duke of Sully. But, despite this, he was assassinated by a Catholic fanatic, Ravaillac, in 1610.

During the reign of Elizabeth I, 1558—1603, England continued to hold itself aloof from the religious wars. Elizabeth choked the claims of the Catholics, as well as those of the Puritans, to the benefit of the only English church.

When her Catholic cousin, Mary Stuart, Queen of Scotland, was banished from her kingdom by her own subjects, she came to Elizabeth for asylum. But Elizabeth, distrustful of her cousin's motives, had her thrown into prison and kept her there for eighteen years before having her beheaded.

Now England began to take advantage of her sea-power, and also began to concentrate much more on sheep raising in order to expand the textile industry. English mastery on the high seas was asserted by sailors like Hawkins and Drake, as they gave chase to the Spanish vessels transporting precious metals from America.

Doctor Faustus

England supported the Netherlands in their bid for independence, fighting with them against Spain. The Spaniards—who had gained a naval victory against the Turks at Lepanto in 1571, where an unknown sailor named Cervantes was wounded—determined to chastise the English. The Invincible Armada took to the sea and met the English fleet in the English Channel. The enemies opposed each other for days in a great sea battle but, outclassed by the superior vessels and gunnery of the British, the Spaniards were in retreat when they encountered a terrible tempest which destroyed the remainder of their fleet.

Elizabeth never married. For this reason Drake, when he conquered part of

Mary Stuart

101

Michel de Montaigne (1533-1592), the greatest writer and thinker of the 16th century. He was the author of the *Essays* which reflected his desire for self-knowledge, his responses to his wide reading, his observations of men and his experience of life. His frankness and self-appraisal give his essays vitality and conviction.

BELOW, FROM TOP TO BOTTOM: Ladies' costumes from the time of Francis I; costumes from the reign of Charles IX, and men's costumes from the time of Henry IV. In the 16th century, courtiers wore very sensible and elegant clothes. In France, there were more fashions than there were monarchs.

BELOW, LEFT: Ivan the Terrible, a bloodthirsty monarch, was a very clever head of state. He put an end to the power of the *boyars* or nobles, and enlarged Russia, which after his reign came under world consideration as a great power. His son, Fyodor, a weak-minded man, succeeded him. Power passed into the hands of Boris Godunov, (RIGHT) who, on Fyodor's death — he was probably poisoned — was proclaimed Tsar. The figure of this usurper, who in his turn died of poison, provided the inspiration for the play *Boris Godunov* by Alexander Pushkin and also for the famous opera by Mussorgsky.

BELOW: The stronghold of the Kremlin, seat of the tsars of Russia, and home today of the Soviet government. The first building was rebuilt in the 12th century but was enlarged considerably by Italian craftsmen in the 17th century.

The defeat of the ' invincible ' Armada

Henry IV renouncing the Protestant doctrines

A microscope (1590)

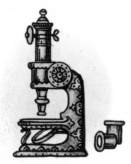

The discovery of the
islands of Spitsbergen

The Globe Theatre,
London

the American continent, named it Virginia in honour of his queen. One day Elizabeth received a proposal of marriage which appeared highly comical to her. It came from a terrible brute who ruled over Russia, 1533—1584, and who was justly named Ivan the Terrible. Brought up in the midst of intrigues and assassinations—for eight years he had been a witness to the death of his mother by poisoning—he had seen terrible sights in the torture chambers, torments and punishments which had turned his heart into stone. Having experienced all this, Ivan IV was a complicated character who combined great fervour and devotion with exceptional cruelty. He ruled over a country that was appallingly backward. The peasants lived in one-room *isbas*, or huts, built one on top of the other like saucepans. They were their master's slaves, and he could sell them, punish them with traditional Russian torture methods, even kill them. Ivan established new taxes and carried on a bitter feud against the Russian nobles, the *boyars*, and against the middle-class people of the trading towns. He conquered Estonia and opened the door to the Caspian Sea, thus gaining himself another title, that of Builder of the Russian Empire.

At the same time, another terrible despot, Akbar the Great, 1568—1586, was unifying the Mogul empire. At the age of twenty years he assumed supreme and sole authority in the land. He was, like Ivan, secretive and subject to formidable rages. Throughout his reign he waged war and conquered territories for his empire. He lived in an ostentatious court: around him were poets, wrestlers, falconers, slaves and eunuchs, and five thousand women, each one having her own apartment and servant. His stables were vaster than those of Elizabeth of England. He did not know how to read or write, but he had an infallible memory. In 1575, a house of worship was built at his command, in which he brought together the representatives of every religious denomination, from Mohammedans to Portuguese Jesuits, and he allowed freedom of worship to all religions in his empire. In 1579, he proclaimed himself God's personal representative.

It was at this period that Persia knew its last splendour. Shah Abbas the Great had created an artillery with the aid of the English and he gained a series of victories against the Turks. He engaged men from many nations to establish a police force which would be safer than that provided by the tribal recruits. He imposed taxes on goods, prosecuted thieves and bribed the Christian merchants by giving them privileges. He reserved for himself the monopoly

A shogun, Japanese feudal lord

Johannes Kepler

Don Quixote

Lope de Vega

of selling the silk, which the English bought from him. He opened schools, one in every district. He built mosques and wonderful palaces at Isfahan, giving grand banquets to which he invited European and Chinese traders. His favourite sport was polo, which the English adopted. In all Islam, Persian is the language of literature. But not all his deeds were praiseworthy. He caused his four sons to be blinded, and he ordained that the royal princes should be raised in the harem, in the company of females and eunuchs. This he did so that they might never prove a challenge to his power. All his energies and schemes, however, could not save the kingdom which, after the death of Shah Abbas in 1629, fell into decadence and was invaded by the Turks, the Afghans and the Russians.

Elizabeth was a terrible queen, but she was certainly the queen deserved by a country of young, turbulent savages. For London, which with its 200,000 inhabitants was then the largest city in the world, swarmed with shopkeepers, apprentices, drunks, pickpockets and beggars—14,000 beggars were counted in 1594.

The English were then beginning to acquire the love of comfort which they have since cherished. They had then, at least in the south, their mattresses and their fireplaces. In the wealthy houses they would spread a layer of reeds on the ground to protect the hem of their garments from the coal-dust. The English ate often and well, meat and deer; they drank wines imported from France and Portugal, and beer which had been introduced from the Netherlands where it was very popular. Fashion dealt with extravagances: embroidered waistcoats were worn, garters of gold and silver, ruffs so big that their wearers needed spoons as long as forearms in order to partake of their soup. Elizabeth possessed sixty wigs; Mary Stuart, in prison, changed her wig every day.

The English developed a new love of the theatre. Before Elizabeth, actors played their roles in the forecourts of inns, but in 1601 London had four public theatres, three private theatres, six companies of actors and the greatest dramatist of all time, William Shakespeare. In fact, the English people loved the theatre so much that an edict of 1591 forbade any performances on Thursdays in order to reserve that day for bear-fighting.

Because of the constant feuds between themselves, the Japanese lords were

The Dutch settle in Djakarta

An episode from the war in the Netherlands, the taking of a town by the Spaniards, from an engraving of the time. The war which the seven Protestant provinces of the north of Flanders waged against the Spaniards ended in their victory and, in 1648, the founding of the independent state of Holland.

BELOW: The high altar in Saint Peter's basilica in Rome, the work of Bernini. This artist was the principal Italian representative of baroque art, which was characterised by its grandeur of scale and its movement, obtained by curved and broken lines and by sumptuous decoration.

LEFT: The map shows the route followed by the Invincible Armada which skirted the British Isles and rejoined the Channel where it suffered a disastrous defeat.

BELOW: *The Calling of Saint Matthew* by Michelangelo Caravaggio in the church of Saint Louis of France, in Rome. Michelangelo was one of the most representative artists of the baroque style, his work being marked by his simplicity of composition and his use of light and shade effects.

Baroque style window

Galileo

Rubens

A messenger in 1615

The Jesuits in Paraguay

almost completely exterminated. This allowed the re-establishment of a central power—not the power of an emperor who was only there for decorum, but the power of the *shogun*, who was a sort of mayor of the palace. Between 1582 and 1598, the shogun was called Hideyoshi. He twice attempted to conquer Korea and China, but in vain. It was much too large a piece of land, and Japan had to wait three centuries before it established itself in these countries.

But Hideyoshi pacified Japan, and after him one of his companions, Tokugawa Ieyasu, settled at Edo—the future Tokyo—where his family were to govern for 270 years.

Japan went through a kind of Renaissance. As in France, the castles were not fortresses any more but sumptuous residences with keeps of four to six stories.

At this time, ceramic art, which we use today for colourful tea services, appeared. This was when Francis Xavier arrived in Japan. He was received by great lords and he had only been there a few years when half a million Japanese were baptised.

A celebrated, almost blind, strolling singer was the first Jesuit of the yellow race. This surprising success had a good reason! The *shogun* made use of Christianity to weaken the power of the Buddhist monks who were, he thought, becoming too strong and independent.

A Jesuit called Japan the " blossoming garden of God ". But the Christians were quickly disappointed in their hopes. As soon as the *shogun* no longer feared a Buddhist rebellion the " blossoming garden of God " withered as rapidly as it had flourished.

The seventeenth century in Europe, a time that is too easily thought of as stable, calm and classical, began with the effervescence of baroque. The baroque man thought himself different from all others, and his art was unlike anything that had gone before.

The word baroque comes probably from the Portuguese word *barroco*, meaning irregular pearls. In art, it was a luxurious, irrational, gaudy and heavy style, which reflected the mood of the unbalanced times. The literary heroes of this era were Cervantes' *Don Quixote* and Corneille's *Le Cid*. Baroque also came to the fore in the domain of the painter: Rubens is the most renowned example. Churches in the baroque style were ornate with

The landing of the Pilgrim Fathers at Massachusetts

The ' defenestration ' of Prague

garlands, palms and crowns and sculptures of crocodiles, hares and storks. The most celebrated monument of this kind is Saint Peter's Basilica in Rome.

Discoveries in science upset the Bible version of the creation of man out of earth. A physician, William Harvey, discovered how blood circulates in the human body.

Kepler, the German astronomer, introduced his theories, which were later to aid Isaac Newton in his principle of the Laws of Gravity. Galileo, another astronomer, but an Italian, revived the idea of Copernicus that the earth revolves around the sun.

Summoned by the Pope to retract this ' heresy ', he consented, thinking aside to himself that this would not prevent the earth from turning!

In 1582, Pope Gregory XIII reformed the Julian calendar, making one year in four a leap year. This Gregorian calendar was accepted by the whole of Europe, except the Russians and the Turks.

Black slaves in North America

The baroque heroes did not practise very many Christian virtues. But it was about this period that Saint Vincent de Paul appeared on the scene. A son of poor peasants from Poui, a village in Gascony, he had been captured by Berber pirates and sold as a slave in Tunis in 1605. After converting one of his masters back to Christianity, he succeeded in escaping. In 1622, he became chaplain to the galley slaves in order to help these unfortunate men " attached forever in chains, crawling with vermin and almost eaten away by decay and infection ". Later, he instituted the orders of the Sisters of Charity and the Daughters of Charity and many great hospitals for foundlings or maltreated children.

Cardinal
Richelieu

The opposition between the Catholic and Protestant religions continued unabated and was the cause of much bloodshed. A spark rekindled hostilities in Prague in 1618. The Emperor, having guaranteed religious freedom to Bohemia, failed to keep his promise.

Jakob
Böehme

The Bohemian patriots and the Emperor's emissaries met together in the castle of Prague. Three of the Emperor's emissaries were hurled out of the castle window, but they were not killed, for they fell into the moat which

The city of Prague with the castle of Hradschin, where the ' defenestration ' took place.

OPPOSITE PAGE: **Detail from a landscape by Peter Paul Rubens. As he matured, this painter depicted more and more the simplicity of the pastoral life which he loved.**

BELOW: **A manuscript written by Galileo on the discovery of four of Jupiter's moons in 1610. He observed that the moons revolved around Jupiter and he called them the Medici moons, in honour of the grand duke Cosmo II. Galileo was responsible for incalculable progress in astronomy and mathematics.**

Saint Vincent de Paul

Saint Peter's Basilica in Rome

Discovery of the circulatory system

Gustavus Adolphus II of Sweden

Wallenstein

was full of leaves. This ' defenestration ' of Prague was the signal for the beginning of a war that went on for so long that it is generally known as the Thirty Years' War.

The Emperor, supported by the Catholic League, at first achieved success against the Protestant princes at the battle of White Hill, near Prague, in 1620. The Danes intervened in vain. But the Swedes, led by their king, Gustavus Adolphus, 1611—1632, and supported by France and the united provinces of the Netherlands, won many brilliant victories. However, unfortunately for them, Gustavus was killed on the day of his victory at Lützen, in 1632, and the Protestants soon had to yield to the Emperor.

Then France openly intervened, but this move brought her much trouble. A Spanish army from the Netherlands arrived almost at the gates of Paris. The situation was saved by the great French generals, Turenne and Condé.
After the victories of Rocroi, in 1643, and Lens, in 1648, the Emperor was compelled to sign the Peace of Westphalia: two treaties, one of Münster and one of Osnabrück. The treaties confirmed religious freedom for the Protestants and the independence of the united provinces of the Netherlands and Switzerland. France gained Alsace, excepting Strasbourg and Mulhouse. The Empire was considerably weakened and France appeared as the premier power in Europe. Meanwhile the struggle continued between France and Spain. France was impeded by the *Frondes*, or minor revolutions of the *Parlement* and lords, who harried the French monarchy. In 1659, France gained the provinces of Artois and Roussillon at the Peace of the Pyrenees. Louis XIV married Maria Theresa, the daughter of Philip IV of Spain.
England, too, was in a state of upheaval. King Charles I, because of his leanings towards despotism and Catholicism, provoked civil war in 1642.

Charles' supporters, known as Cavaliers because they were mostly gentlemen, were opposed by the Puritans, known as Roundheads, whose leader was Oliver Cromwell. The king's supporters were defeated at the battles of Marston Moor, in 1644, and Naseby, in 1645. Charles took refuge in the Highlands of Scotland but he was handed over to Parliament by the Scots. A special court was nominated to try the king, of whom half refused to serve.

Production of an opera by Monteverdi in Venice

Rembrandt

Charles refused to plead, denying the jurisdiction of the court, but he was condemned for treason and executed in Whitehall before a great crowd on 30 January, 1649.

Parliament at this time was known as the Rump Parliament, as Cromwell had expelled all the ministers who were not in agreement with him. Cromwell proclaimed a republic known as the Commonwealth, but which was in effect a military dictatorship.

The Irish people revolted against him and, as a result, thousands of Catholic landowners were massacred by the ruthless Roundheads.

Cromwell dissolved parliament after parliament and finally dispensed with them altogether. He took the title of " Lord Protector of the Republic of England, Scotland and Ireland ".

Cardinal Mazarin

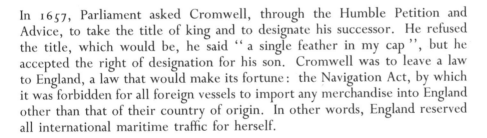

In 1657, Parliament asked Cromwell, through the Humble Petition and Advice, to take the title of king and to designate his successor. He refused the title, which would be, he said " a single feather in my cap ", but he accepted the right of designation for his son. Cromwell was to leave a law to England, a law that would make its fortune: the Navigation Act, by which it was forbidden for all foreign vessels to import any merchandise into England other than that of their country of origin. In other words, England reserved all international maritime traffic for herself.

Torricelli and the barometer

32 inches

We have seen France battling against the Empire and against Spain. Internally, Louis XIII's Prime Minister, Cardinal Richelieu, was effectively employed in reducing the claims for independence which the lords and Protestants were continually making. Richelieu died in 1642, and his king the following year, leaving the regency to Queen Anne of Austria and the power to Cardinal Mazarin.

English fashion in the 17th century

It was at this time that the nobles, allied to members of the *Parlement*, began a series of armed rebellions which were called by the derisive name, the *Frondes*. But, child's play though they were, these rebellions lasted for four years, spreading over all the country and causing ruin, famine and epidemics. At Rouen, 17,000 people died in one year. The hospital was so full that it was necessary to crowd " eight or ten people in the same bed, and sometimes there was only one left alive among seven or eight dead bodies ". The peace

LEFT: Charles I of the House of Stuart, a detail from a painting by Van Dyck. This unfortunate monarch was condemned to death by his subjects, a victim of his own conception of absolutism.

ABOVE: Philip IV of Spain, painted by Velázquez. Cultured and intelligent, but weak, Philip committed the error of joining forces with the Hapsburgs of Austria in the Thirty Years War, which led to the unfortunate loss of the United Provinces of the Netherlands and the beginning of a long period of war against France. When it finished he had to recognise France as being the premier power in Europe. It was during his reign, too, that Portugal separated itself from Spain and became independent.

ABOVE: One of the many portraits of his wife, Saskia, by Rembrandt. After Saskia's death, the people that the artist painted, generally the quiet Flemish bourgoisie, were presented in a more and more expressive way, often shrouded in dramatic and mysterious light.

ABOVE: The Queen's House at Greenwich.

LEFT: The Banqueting Hall in Whitehall, London. These two palaces were considered to be very revolutionary in England, where Tudor and perpendicular Gothic styles predominated, classicism appearing only as elements of decoration. Their designer, Inigo Jones, was influenced by the work of Antonio Palladio and other Italian architects.

A surgeon operating

Monastery of the Dalai Lama
at Lhasa

Baroque church

Violin maker of Cremona

The Thirty Years' War

of the interior was gradually re-established, and international peace was strengthened by the Treaty of the Pyrenees before Mazarin's death in 1661. Louis XIV was going to reign alone.

In the same year, a seven-year old child ascended the Chinese throne: K'ang-Hsi, who was to reign for sixty-two years. Before him the Ming dynasty had been in steady decline. Princes and nobles used to seize the lands and exploit the peasants, who then fled and became bandits or pirates. China, at that time, was living on her past, remembering her old customs and giving herself up to anarchy. The inevitable consequences occurred: the country was invaded by a sturdy race of hunters and foresters, the Manchus. K'ang-Hsi was one of these, a young Manchu prince, and destined to be a very great king. To support his policies he had at his disposal not only an army of tough, courageous men, but also the scientific knowledge of the Jesuits, who had come to the country in the hope of converting the Chinese. Their knowledge of astronomical science helped the Emperor to establish an accurate calendar, which was really essential in China where life was carefully regulated on the paths of the stars. The priests' science also brought him a more material help: they invented for him a piece of artillery which enabled him to quell victoriously the attacks of the Russians.

In recognition of the Jesuits' valuable help, the Emperor proclaimed two edicts of tolerance for Catholicism, which then made rapid progress in China. But, at the same time, the Jesuits adopted several Chinese rites so as to be better understood by their converts. Pope Clement XI condemned these rites in 1704, and the Emperor forbade the practice of Christianity in China.

At the same time, there reigned in India a great-grandson of Akbar, Aurangzeb (1658—1707), who was himself a very great king, contemporary with Louis XIV of France. It is true to say that he was the last of the great Moguls, for he did all that there was to do to make himself great, and to make himself the last of the line. He murdered his brothers and imprisoned his father. He was deeply religious, but he believed neither in men nor their virtues. He was a despot. He himself said: "I am lord of the world and in my shadow men must lie as though under a parasol." But this parasol did not provide any shelter from the rain. He conquered Tibet, Deccan and the kingdom of Golconda, and carried off all their treasure.

Delhi, where he held his court, was the scene of great pageantry. His religious fanaticism incited him to destroy the schools and temples of the infidels,

116

Guericke's experiments with atmospheric pressure

that is to say, all those who were not orthodox Mohammedans. So many wars and so many persecutions naturally led to revolts. He crushed them all, but after him his sons were to fight amongst themselves and the country was divided.

It was in Aurangzeb's reign that the French established a base at Pondicherry and the English settled in Madras and Bombay: the first steps towards Franco-English rivalry in India, which would develop in the 18th century, at the same time as their rivalry in America.

In America, the Portuguese, masters of Brazil, had to protect the country from French merchants and pirates who came to trade with the Indians. The Portuguese were quite numerous enough to succeed in this: more than 40,000 already at the beginning of the 17th century, with 15,000 black slaves that they had brought over from Africa. The wealth of the country came from the red-tinted wood that grew there, called brazilwood, and from the sugar cane.

The white people and the *mamelucos*—those born of marriages between white men and black women—thought themselves quite authorised to treat the Indians as slaves. The Jesuits, therefore, took the Indians under their protection, and they began to cultivate sugar cane, cotton, tobacco, cocoa and spices, thus making embarrassing competition for the colonists. Little by little they were pushed back towards Uruguay.

These Jesuits were engaged in conducting a remarkable experiment in Paraguay, with the authority of the king of Spain. Their state was founded on a basis of collective ownership, from the fields to the printing workshops and the foundries for bells and cannons.

The Indians, who were called *Guaranis*, had two days of the week to cultivate the field which they had been conceded. The other four days they worked on the lands of the community. On Sundays they played football, shot at targets and attended horse races and concerts. They were provided in abundance with provisions, they had all that they wanted, but nothing actually belonged to them. This was an exceptional form of colonisation which caused the other Indians, who were exploited by the colonists, to realise even more the failings of their own civilisation.

The colonists were alarmed at the activities of the Jesuits and, in 1767, King

Execution of
Charles I of England

Descartes

Molière

Thomas Hobbes

ABOVE: An episode from
the Thirty Years' War,
the surrender of Breda,
painted by Velazquez.

RIGHT: The famous astro-
nomical observatory at
Greenwich as it appeared
in the 18th century, from
an engraving of that time.
Founded in 1675 by King
Charles II, it was trans-
ferred in the 1950's to
Herstmonceaux Castle in
Sussex, where the air was
clearer than in the city,
allowing more accurate
observations.

Louis XIV crossing the Rhine

Oliver Cromwell

The first magic lantern

French style garden

French loom

Charles III of Spain issued a decree banishing the Jesuits from the entire Spanish Empire.

In Mexico, the Spaniards possessed vast domains on which they made the Indians work. These Indians were all converted to Catholicism and spoke Spanish. The biggest cathedral of the century was built in Mexico.
In 1620, English Puritans had sailed in the ship the *Mayflower*, and landed in North America, where they founded the first states—New England, Massachusetts, Connecticut. This was the nucleus of British colonisation. To-day, American social climbers like to claim descent from these immigrants.

Little by little, the English colonists journeyed down the length of the coast of the United States, fighting the Indians in order to take their lands. Oliver Cromwell's victory in England caused another type of people to emigrate—the gentlemen who had been defeated. These men established themselves in the South—Virginia, Maryland, Carolina and Georgia—where they set up plantations of rice, cotton and tobacco, using negro slaves imported from Africa for labour. In the North the Puritans were in control. In the centre, immigrants of mixed nationalities were settled.
Thus the thirteen initial colonies were instituted. Each one had a governor appointed by the King of England, but they elected their own assemblies to ratify laws, decide on the budget and determine the governor's salary. Englishmen took the privileges of their mother country over to America.

France was not taking much interest in these great voyages of discovery. Nevertheless, Francis I supported three expeditions of Jacques Cartier up the Saint Lawrence as far as the island of Montreal. The economic crisis of the 17th century urged France to imitate her neighbours. By an admirable system of navigation the French penetrated the continent, discovering the Saint Lawrence, the Great Lakes, the Mississippi and journeying far beyond the English. After Champlain had founded Quebec, the French spread their domination over the Great Lakes, Ohio and Illinois, from where Cavelier de La Salle sailed down the Mississippi to the mouths of the river in 1682 and offered Louis XIV a country in his own name: Louisiana. The English on the coast found themselves completely encircled by the French.

The Palace of Versailles, before the building of the Hall of Mirrors (1679)

Artificial canal

At the same time, the French occupied the Lesser Antilles, abandoned by the Spaniards, and developed sugar cane plantations there. But for the moment sugar did not interest France as much as the valuable furs of Canada.

For the most part the French people, unlike the English, had no wish to leave their mother country. So every now and then, tramps, convicts and prostitutes were shipped out from France to people these immense territories stretching from Canada as far as Louisiana. But, fortunately, the number of vagabonds in the world is proportionately small so, at the end of the 17th century, there were only 12,000 lost souls in these vast lands.

Emperor K'ang-Hsi

In all the colonies, Portuguese, Spanish, English or French, the 'exclusive system' reserved the monopoly of trade for the home country. The trading was three-sided: merchandise was exported to Africa where negro slaves were taken on board, to be shipped back to the colonies, from where the boats sailed back to their home country with the products of the lands. The profits from these enterprises were enormous.

A cathedral in Mexico

Louis XIV, whose personal reign began in 1661, wanted France to be thought of as the premier nation in Europe. Jean Colbert, his Minister of Finance, gave him much powerful aid. He endeavoured to increase the collection of taxes without increasing the taxes themselves. He tried to abolish the squandering of government funds, and developed the leather, linen and iron industries. He instituted the manufacture of porcelain, mirrors and tapestries, and French goods gained a reputation for quality. He cut a canal across the south of France to join the Mediterranean with the Atlantic. He gave France the most powerful navy of that time—though the English were to sink part of it in a battle during the War of the League of Augsburg in 1692.

Meanwhile, Louis XIV waged war against the Spanish Netherlands, then against Holland. The Peace of Nijmegan in 1678 established his leadership, and he deserves to be called Louis the Great.

In 1682, he moved into his palace at Versailles, which had been built over a period of twenty years by 30,000 labourers. Louis himself directed the building of the palace, which cost him about three hundred million gold francs. It also cost thousands of human lives, for the land that was moved to

Spanish fashion of the 17th century

Surrounded by vignettes and quotations on peace, virtue and progress, and crushing Babylon and Error beneath his feet, Oliver Cromwell, Lord Protector, appears on this engraving of 1658 as the 'Emblem of the long awaited and now attained Liberty and Happiness of England.'

Louis XIV, the Grand Monarch, from a painting by Rigaud in the Louvre museum.

ABOVE, RIGHT: The pool of Apollo at the foot of the *Tapis Vert*, or green carpet, in the park of Versailles. The palace and park of Versailles were masterpieces of Louis XIV.

BELOW: Crowds cheer Charles II, son of the executed king, as he lands at Dover to be crowned king of England. In 1660, a new period of English history began, known as the Restoration.

A fort of the Hudson Bay Company

John Amos Comenius

Isaac Newton

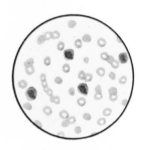

Discovery of red corpuscles in blood

The war in Holland

cut the canal caused a kind of plague. Marie de Sévigné, the French writer, said in 1678 that every night " carts full of bodies " could be seen around the town.

The king gave ostentatious feasts for his courtiers, who applauded the operas of Lully and the comedies of Molière. Each courtier had a particular function to perform in the palace, all of which were carried out with strict etiquette. It was a much coveted right to be able to present the king with his shirt or his wig. The king's rising and bedding were performed with great ceremony. During the reign of Louis, classical art blossomed and France produced great artists like Poussin, and great writers such as Racine, Bossuet, La Bruyére, Boileau, La Fontaine and Marie de Sévigné.

While Louis XIV was settling himself in his palace at Versailles, 200,000 Turks were besieging Vienna (1683).
This was the last menace of the Ottoman Empire, which was rapidly declining. The Polish king, John Sobieski, hastened to the rescue of the Empire and pushed back the Turks. The Ottoman Empire was no longer a threat.

In England, during the years of Cromwell's domination, the Puritans were detested. The Stuarts took advantage of this hate to return Charles II to the throne in 1660. This Restoration began very badly: in 1665 the Great Plague of London claimed 100,000 victims. The following year the great fire ravaged London.
Under a kindly exterior, Charles II was a lazy and hypocritical king. He was suspected of sympathising with Catholicism, and he did in fact make a secret alliance with Louis XIV, with the intention of restoring Catholicism to England.

In 1673, the English Parliament passed the Test Act, which excluded Catholics from all public functions and compelled all holders of office to take oaths of allegiance and receive Communion according to Anglican rites. Now the king's brother, James II, who was also his heir, was a Catholic. The country became split on the question of the Exclusion Bill, which was an attempt by Parliament to prohibit the succession of the Catholic brother in the absence

The Turks in Vienna

The astronomer Halley

of children of the king. Those who supported the king were known as Tories, and supporters of Parliament were called Whigs. So the two great English political parties were born.

Charles II died in 1685. Immediately his brother, James II, followed a Catholic policy, directed by the king of France, which stirred up his Protestant subjects against him. Some of them invited William of Orange, the Stadholder of Holland, whose wife Mary was James' daughter, to come over to England to intervene. William landed, and without any blows being struck, James fled to France in 1688.

William and Mary were proclaimed joint rulers by Parliament, and they accepted the Declaration of Rights which guaranteed the prerogative of Parliament. By this peaceful revolution England was ruled, from that day, by a constitutional monarchy.

William Penn

Russia, where Peter the Great reigned between 1672 and 1725, was far removed from the spirit of Western Europe. The tsar, a giant 7½ feet tall, undertook with unflagging energy to open his country to the Western civilisation. Incognito, he made a fact-finding journey to Amsterdam, London, Venice and Vienna. Later he visited Versailles. Having decided to establish a navy, he directed the shipyard himself, and built a boat with his own hands. In 1703, he decided to found a city, which would become Saint Petersburg, his 'window on the West'. Doubtless taking the view that the habit makes the monk, he forbade his subjects to wear beards and long coats; he himself cut the beards and coats of the *boyars*. Through the Baltic, with the help of his fleet, he established the closest possible contacts with the West of Europe. It is not possible in a single reign to totally change such a vast country, but Peter the Great succeeded in westernising the upper areas of Russia. This untiring man, who was always risking his own life, dived into the frozen waters of a river to help save some soldiers from drowning. He caught cold and died on 28 January, 1725.

The Huguenots in Holland

In France, Louis XIV increased his absolute power. Wishing that all his subjects should practise his own religion, he attempted to convert the Protestants to Catholicism by persecution, notably by billeting troops in their houses. In 1685, thinking that he had broken their spirit, he revoked the Edict of Nantes, by which Henry IV had extended tolerance to the

John Locke

Painting by Van der Meulen, illustrating t[...]
siege of Besancon during the Franco-Du[...]
wars.

OPPOSITE PAGE, TOP: Prints illustrating life [...]
China under the Ch'ing dynasty (1644-191[...]
The print on the left shows the sumptuo[...]
palace of a mandarin. The mandarins we[...]
leading citizens, holding the highest milita[...]
and civil offices. The print on the right illu[...]
trates a pagoda on a bridge, in the region [...]
Fukien.

ABOVE: John III Sobieski, King of Poland. H[...]
defeated the Turks at the Second Siege of Vienn[...]

LEFT: Isaac Newton, born in England in 164[...]
the year Galileo died.

OPPOSITE PAGE, BOTTOM: In November 168[...]
William Penn formed a treaty of friendship wit[...]
the Indians: the only treaty, according t[...]
Voltaire, which was never sealed and neve[...]
broken. A Quaker missionary, Penn created i[...]
Pennsylvania a Christian state founded on th[...]
principles of his sect.

Peter the Great in Holland

The tsar, Peter the Great

Prince Eugene

Belvedere Castle

Charles XII of Sweden

Protestant religion. Hundreds of thousands of Protestants emigrated to England, Holland and even Prussia, where they were to make Berlin wealthy.

The Empire, now rid of the menace of the Turks, rose up against Louis XIV's claim to leadership, Spain, Holland and William III forming the nucleus of the coalition. The war that followed was known as the War of the League of Augsburg, and France lost her fleet in a naval battle in 1692. The Peace of Ryswick, in 1697, put an early end to the hostilities, but France suffered a decisive defeat.

But things were different in the war of the Spanish Succession in which, between 1702 and 1714, France struggled alone against all of Europe. This war was so named because it started when the grandson of Louis XIV, the Duke d'Anjou, accepted the succession to the Spanish throne when Charles II of Spain died without an heir. But the other powers in Europe had no wish to see Louis XIV as master of Madrid. France was on the brink of collapse when she saved herself at the last moment by the victory of the Duke of Villars over the Imperial army at Denain in 1712.
All these wars cost France dear. A terrible misery reigned over the country and the French people came to hate Louis XIV. When he died, on 1 September, 1715, the provinces, according to the historian, the Duke of Saint-Simon, "jumped for joy", and the people "gave thanks to God".

The end of the 17th century was also marked by events, which, though not political, were not any the less important in the history of the world.
One of these, in the scientific field, was the discovery in 1683 by Isaac Newton, an Englishman, of the laws of universal gravity. The legend goes that Newton actually discovered the laws when he observed an apple falling from a tree.
Another event, in the philosophic and social field, was the publication, in 1689, again in England, of a book by John Locke, whose title alone was a declaration of war on the despotism of the continent: *Letter on Tolerance*. "Men," said Locke, "are all born free and equal to one another. They are led by reason which shows them their natural rights of freedom, property and family. In defence of these rights, rebellion is justified."

Porcelain factory in Europe

The Berlin Academy
of Sciences

Leibniz

The Duke of Marlborough

The first oil light

All of the 18th century is marked by the rivalry between England and France. At first the competition was peaceful. Besides, the financial state of the two countries was not such that any fighting could be promoted.

In France, the Duke of Orléans, regent on the death of Louis XIV, printed bank-notes with the help of the Scottish financier, John Law. To make them acceptable, he assured the country that they could exchange the notes for gold and silver. But the gold, which the banks disposed of, did not represent more than five hundred million francs, and Orléans circulated three thousand million in notes. Bankruptcy was inevitable.

The West Indies dominated the politics of that time. France and England contended for them, as well as for India, where anarchy had reigned since the death of Aurangzeb, in 1707. It was during this period of anarchy that the English and the French established their domination, by expanding the power of their trading companies.

Whilst France fell into decay, Prussia, governed by Frederick William, flourished. Frederick I had but one aim: to create a Prussian army. He did so by establishing an obligatory military service, the first in Europe, and by imposing a severe government over the lives of his people. This army, in which Frederick took too great a pride to risk it in battle, was used by his son Frederick II in 1740 to attack Marie-Thérèse of Austria when she came to the throne.

Marie-Thérèse was then twenty-three. She was sprightly, gay and intelligent. She enjoyed life to the full and considered her status as a sacred gift entrusted to her by God. Her activities as empress did not prevent her from playing the rôle of mother to her six children. Frederick said of her, " She is a great woman who has done credit to her sex ".

Frederick II was not the only adversary of Marie-Thérèse. The Bavarians, Saxons and French eventually saw the need to overthrow the house of Austria. France, who allied herself with Prussia, was also to fight England for seventy years. But the real stakes of this war lay over the seas.

France invaded the Netherlands. To come to their aid, Marie-Thérèse launched an offensive against Alsace. Louis XV left for Metz to assume control of the defence, but was taken ill there. It was then that he became known as

The first king of Prussia, Frederick I. He was already Elector of Brandenburg when he was named king by the emperor and, in order to fulfil his ambition, he had himself crowned amid a spectacular ceremony.

BELOW: The battle of Poltava, where Peter the Great defeated his rival Charles XII of Sweden. When the enemy army invaded his country, the tsar adopted the traditional Russian tactic of drawing the enemy far from their store camps and forcing them to accept the battle in the most unfavourable position.

РАСКОЛЬНІКЪ ГОВОРИТЪ СЛУШАІ ЦЫРЮЛЬНИКЪ Я БОРОДЫ СТРИЧЬ НЕ ХОЧУ ВОТЪ ГЛЕДИ Я НА ТЕБЯ СКОРО КАРАУЛЪ ЗАКРЮ

ЦЫРЮЛЬНІЙКЪ ХО ЧЕТЪ РАСКОЛЬНІКУ БОРОДУ СТРИЧЬ .

Contrary to traditions but acting from a desire to enter into European politics, Peter the Great sought to modernise and westernise the old Russia. Using European architects, he constructed, in a very short time, the town of St. Petersburg.

ABOVE: A caricature of that time shows the tsar with a barber's apron, scissors in hand, cutting the beard of an unworthy Russian noblemen.

OPPOSITE, LEFT: The Winter Palace and the Peterhof Palace, works of the Italian Rastrelli. In order to force his subjects to adopt European customs, Peter the Great had to impose harsh measures, such as stationing policemen on the roadways to cut the excessively long beards of the rebels.

A sitting of Parliament in England

Cyrillic characters

Москва	Moscow
Киев	Kiev
Одесса	Odessa
Тифлис	Tiflis

Baroque architecture in Sicily

Gibraltar

The slave-trade

Louis the Beloved.

In 1745, Marshal Maurice de Saxe, a German commanding the French forces, won a great victory over the British, Austrian, Dutch and Hanoverian armies at Fontenoy.

In 1748, the French seized the United Provinces of the Netherlands, but the treaty of Aix-la-Chapelle gave nothing to France. Madame de Pompadour, favourite of the king since 1745, told the French diplomats when they were leaving to negotiate the treaty of Aix-la-Chapelle, " Do not return without a peace settlement, the King wants no more war ". She had a great influence over the king and also amongst his financiers. The allies of Louis XV received what they coveted. Louis, without anyone asking it of him, restored all his conquests: the Netherlands, Savoy, the county of Nice, even the spoils of war. The people adopted a saying, " Nonsensical as peace ".

Why had Louis XV signed this peace? Because the financiers wanted it, in order that they might peacefully carry out trade in the West Indies.

The settlers of New England brought to the French islands meats, building materials, and all the necessities for cultivating sugar, whilst the English islands lacked everything. The English merchants themselves dishonestly bought French sugar to send to England. This deceit succeeded in time of peace, but it was feared that it would be disastrous in wartime when the communications would be cut.

Meanwhile the colonies grew, in America, in the valley of the Mississippi, between Canada and Louisiana. Quebec and Montreal became important towns in Canada. New Orleans became a great port in Louisiana. Martinique, Guadeloupe and Santo Domingo continued to flourish, due to their sugar, coffee, tobacco, and cocoa plantations. But the energy of the English statesman, William Pitt, allowed the English to seize from France, in four years, Canada and the French possessions in India that Dupleix had been able to retain. England gained command of the sea.

The treaty of Paris in 1763 completed the downfall of the French colonial empire. But France did not realise the importance of her losses. She concentrated her attention on the Antilles, and the cultivation of sugar cane

English garden and parkland

New Orleans

seemed to her of sufficient commercial interest not to bother herself " about a few acres of ice ", as Voltaire said when speaking of Canada.

England was undergoing a great transformation. She became the country of extensive agricultural properties and of industrial production. Cotton from India, the invention of the flying shuttle which increased the weaving output, and of Wyatt's spinning-machine: these were the basis of the great British capitalism which was being born.

Frederick II (1740—1786), king of Prussia at 28, asserted himself as a great monarch. He was " the sole and universal minister of his monarchy ".

Robinson Crusoe

The French philosophers hailed him as a model of their ideal, " the enlightened despot ". He encouraged immigration, consolidated the monetary system, (the *thaler*, from which the English word *dollar* originated), founded a ' Royal Bank ', and proclaimed freedom of thought in his State.
This friend of philosophers was a great leader. He opposed himself to Austria who supported France, producing a reversal of alliance. He defeated the Austrians in Silesia, but suffered a bloody defeat at Kolin, in June, 1757. His forces were exhausted but, suddenly, Peter III of Russia, who had just come to the throne (1762) and who was an admirer of Frederick—he was German by birth—put his troops at the disposal of the Prussian king. Frederick seized Cassel from the French and overwhelmed the Austrians and the German princes.

George Frederick Handel

Paris, the model of foreign nations, or the French Europe was the title of a short work written by an Italian in 1777 and edited in Paris by the ambassador of Naples. France was then in fact the nation which all others strove to imitate. Her scholars were the admiration of Europe. Lavoisier formulated the laws of chemistry, Buffon wrote his *Natural History*. There was Laplace, Lagrange, Monge, and the French-speaking Swiss Bernouilli family, who greatly contributed to the progress of mathematical principles. Cugnot constructed the first steam vehicle, the Marquis of Jouffroy the first steam boat, and the Montgolfier brothers flew the first hot-air balloon.
Writers called themselves philosophers. " To philosophize ", said Madame

Johann Sebastian Bach

LEFT: Supposed portrait
of Antonio Vivaldi,
famous Venetian com-
poser.

African bronze statue
representing a Portu-
guese soldier.

In 1700, all the great European powers had possessions on the African coast. The principal source of revenue was the slave-trade, practised above all with the American plantation owners.

BELOW: Diagram showing the way in which the slaves were crowded into the boats which transported them.

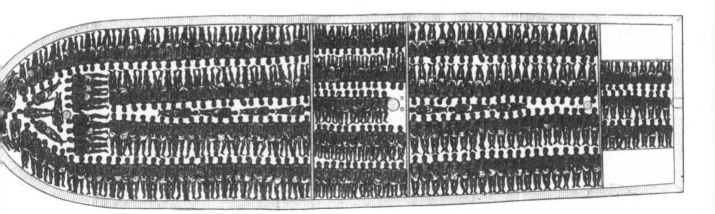

The crossing of the Bering Strait

Leuwenhoeck

An episode from *Gulliver's Travels*

Carl von Linné

Rococo doorway

de Lambert, who had a much frequented salon, " is to render to reason all its dignity and to restore it to its rights. It is to shake off the yoke of opinion and authority ".

Montesquieu, Voltaire, Rousseau and Diderot were European celebrities. Voltaire was the friend of Frederick II who invited him to his court. Catherine II became Diderot's benefactor. Montesquieu's *The Spirit of Laws*, which analysed the divers forms of government, inspired the enlightened monarchs, whilst Rousseau launched revolutionary ideas which the Jacobins were to take up again in 1792. Diderot directed the compilation of *The Encyclopaedia*, which contained contributions from most of the leading French writers of that time and expressed many revolutionary opinions.

The French language was the language of the courts, of scholars and of scientists. It was in French that England and Russia concluded their treaty of alliance, in French that the commercial treaties were signed and, in the Russian court, Catherine II herself used the French language. Frederick II considered that German was a barbarous jargon, and Marie-Thérèse of Austria communicated with her children in French.

The true rulers of society were the women. They held ' salons ' which were frequented by the celebrated men of the era, and where every eminent foreigner aspired to be received. Foreigners flocked to Paris. They met with each other in these salons, and also in the cafés, where they enjoyed the latest fashionable drinks.

France had never been so prosperous nor so charitable. But the Government exempted various classes, such as the clergy and the nobility, from certain taxes, and as a result of these privileges the burden of taxation lay heavily on the middle, peasant and artisan classes. All reform was opposed by the Government and the State ran to ruin.

Catherine II of Russia, wife of the degenerate and insignificant Peter III, became tsarina of Russia in 1763, at the age of 33, after having dethroned her husband and had him secretly assassinated. She pretended that he had died from a brain storm.

Known as Catherine the Great, she was violent, despotic, dissolute, but at the same time intelligent, cultured, gay, courageous and industrious.

136

An abbey in Austria

Freemason

Throughout her reign she was 'the constant sentinel'.

She extorted territories from the Poles and from the Turks to make a still greater Russia. For her, as for Frederick of Prussia, the most urgent task was to colonise her kingdom. She brought thousands of emigrants from Germany to populate the rich, but empty, lands of the Ukraine and of the Volga. Thus two hundred towns and villages were created in southern Russia, of which the most important was Odessa.

The *moujiks*, Russian peasants led by a Cossack named Pougatchev, revolted in 1771. Catherine subdued this revolt, took Pougatchev prisoner, locked him in a cage, sent him to Moscow, had his head cut off, and then had the decapitated corpse quartered.

Catherine was a despot, but she was also a skilful and conscientious ruler. She built towns, opened hospitals and introduced the potato. In 1767, she summoned a commission representative of all classes—except, of course, the serf class, which was numerically much the greatest—and this consultative body issued a code inspired by the ideas of liberty, tolerance and equality: precepts which stemmed from the French philosophers whom Catherine admired.

Marie Thérèsa

Frederick II

The English, impoverished by the Seven Years' War, tried to recoup by imposing taxes on their American colonies.

In 1776, the American Congress proclaimed the Declaration of Rights and Independence of their thirteen colonies under the name of the Republic of the United States. But the English would not agree to this, and the Americans themselves were divided. This situation led to the War of Independence between the Insurgents, commanded by George Washington (1732—1799) and the English, aided by American loyalists. Benjamin Franklin, the inventor of the lightning conductor, received the support of a number of young European nobles, including the famous Marquis de la Fayette, for the defence of the Insurgents' cause.

Franklin's experiment

The English were beaten in Virginia in 1781 by the Americans, commanded

ABOVE: **Two carrying chairs, in the rococo style; that on the left is Neapolitan, and that on the right is Roman.**

RIGHT: **A rococo set with Chinese decorations. The work of F. Juvara, from the Royal Palace at Turin.**

While the principal industries were born in the 18th century, there was also a great revival of interest in the traditional crafts. *On the left* are shown a group of French foundry workers.

Scenes of everyday life in the 18th century.

ABOVE, LEFT: A game of cards, painted by an unknown artist.

RIGHT: A group of people at a theatrical performance. Detail from a painting by G. P. Pannini.

OPPOSITE: An allegorical representation of the 18th century representing horometry. The method of clock-making, which is still employed today, was developed at the court of Louis XIV of France by Christiaan Huygens, who expanded the ideas of Galileo on the swing of the pendulum.

Concert during the rococo period

Voltaire

A scene from *Émile*, by Jean Jacques Rousseau

The residence at Würzburg

Rococo statuette

by General Washington, and by the French, commanded by Admiral de Grasse. Under the Treaty of Versailles, signed in 1783, Britain recognised the independence of the United States up to the Mississippi. Britain kept Gibraltar, but ceded Florida and Minorca to Spain. France recovered Tobago and St. Lucia in the West Indies, as well as Senegal.

The war had been disastrous for Britain, France, Spain and Holland. Even the United States, though successful, was to find that independence had its cares too, as the country embarked on a highly critical and difficult period. In 1787, the United States had established a constitution which appeared ideal to the liberated Europeans and to the Latin Americans. In 1789, George Washington was elected President of the United States.

A liberal wind blew across Europe also, where the ' enlightened despots '— Frederick II of Prussia, Catherine of Russia and even the Holy Roman Emperor, Joseph II, son of Francis I and of Marie-Thérèse (1765—1790)— tried to introduce reforms which would lead to a ' new society '. This spirit of freedom was at work in Geneva, in the Netherlands (now Belgium) and in Holland.

In France also, at the end of Louis XV's reign, the absolute monarchy was attempting reform. Maupeou, an energetic and fearless minister, saw clearly that it was necessary to establish a closer association between the people and the throne.

In the provinces, municipal councillors were in charge of local administration, under the chairmanship of a Mayor, who was appointed by the king. These councillors were appointed by a committee of prominent men, but there was no real system of elected local government. Louis tried in some way to amend this by abolishing hereditary succession to these offices. He dismissed those who opposed his reforms and replaced them with others of more liberal views. He also instituted a system of free justice, forbidding bribes. These reforms were resented by those who managed to wrest profit from disorder and discontent. But Louis was ineffective, succeeding only in making himself unpopular among this section of the people. He died in 1774.

He was succeeded by his grandson, Louis XVI, a man of personal virtue and

The English in India

The University of Columbia

The University of Moscow

Joseph Haydn

Catherine II

good intentions, but a weak ruler who was much influenced and ill-advised by his beautiful wife, the frivolous and extravagant Marie Antoinette. Louis tried to make some reforms, but he ran into opposition from the clergy and nobility, who refused to relinquish their tax immunities. Turgot, Comptroller-General of Finances (1774—1776), attempted such reforms as freeing the corn trade and abolishing the royal *corvée*—forced and unpaid labour on the roads— replacing it by a territorial tax, imposed on all land-owners. But, despite these measures and numerous loans, France's monetary debt trebled during the reign of Louis XVI.

The reform of the monarchy became more and more urgent. The Third Estate—which consisted of commoners, artisans and peasants—were demanding drastic changes.

The active period of the Revolution was precipitated by the financial collapse of the French Government, bled by wars and extravagance.

Compelled by the financial emergency to take extraordinary measures, Louis XVI summoned the States-General on 5 May, 1789; this body had not met since 1614. But, supported by most of the clergy and nobility present as delegates, he refused to give France a constitution. On 20 June, the Third Estate broke away from this Assembly and met in a nearby tennis court. By the famous 'Tennis Court Oath', these deputies resolved to remain there until the establishment of a constitution had been agreed.

Opposed by the king, the Assembly found support in Paris where, on 14 July, the people rose up and seized the Bastille, the state prison and a symbol of despotism.

Revolt spread through the provinces. The peasants plundered and set fire to the castles. During the night of 4 August the National Assembly met and voted the abolition of all feudal rights and privileges. On 26 August it framed a constitution which restricted royal power and stated that sovereignty lay in the hands of the people, declaring that all men were free and equal, in the famous Declaration of the Rights of Man. This was a major step forward; it would seem that revolution might be avoided.

But the king did not really accept the acts of the Assembly. Neither did their verbal passing bring any relief to the hungry or the unemployed, as famine

In the century of light, modern science was born from the ashes of alchemy, thanks to the great scholar Lavoisier. On the left you can see the scales for measuring gases which were taken from his laboratory and are now on display at the Museum of Arts and Crafts in Paris.

ABOVE: A reunion of writers of the French *Encyclopédie*. One can recognise Voltaire, with his hand raised, and, on the left, Diderot, the founder, with D'Alembert, his principal aid. A compilation of essays, the *Encyclopédie* was an effective instrument for spreading new ideas in Europe.

LEFT: Benjamin Franklin, from an etching by G. Galléna. Writer, statesman and scholar, Franklin helped draft the American Declaration of Independence and the Constitution.

OPPOSITE: The French ship *Thésée*, sunk by the English admiral, Hawke. Beaten by the English navy during the Seven Years' War, France lost nearly all her possessions in Asia and America.

Jean Jacques Rousseau, from a crayon drawing by Maurice Quentin de la Tour. Rousseau believed that man should live according to nature, allowing himself to be guided by his instincts and feelings rather than by the tyranny of reason. Men, he held, were born free and equal and it was society that corrupted them. Rousseau's theories and beliefs exerted a profound influence over his period.

Archaeological digs in Italy

The Pantheon

Watt's steam machine

Cook in the Southern seas

spread across the country during that terrible winter.

The revolution now reached a new and violent stage. On 5 October, Louis and his family were forcibly taken from Versailles to Paris. The crowd following the king's carriage cried: " We are bringing back the baker, the baker's wife and the pastrycook's boy ". This was, no doubt, a reference to the alleged remark of Marie Antoinette that if the people had no bread to eat then they should eat cake.

Once again one might have thought that the revolution was ending. The Assembly drew up a constitution. On 14 July, 1790, the anniversary of the taking of the Bastille, there was a celebration, attended by all representatives, in Paris. Louis XVI swore before the Assembly to accept the new constitution.

But under the new constitution the clergy were to come under state control and all church lands were to be taken over by the state. Louis, who was very religious, could not reconcile his conscience to these laws. On the night of 20 June, 1791, he and his family tried to flee beyond the frontier. He hoped to return to France at the head of an army which would dissolve the Assembly. But they were caught at Varennes and brought back to Paris. So, on 30 September, before the Constitution broke up, Louis took a new oath.

During all this time, religious, political, economic and social troubles were tearing France apart. Clergy who would not accept the constitution were being hunted and killed. Famine was widespread. Supporters of the king sought to re-establish an absolute monarchy. The revolutionaries, who had avowed their intention to carry the revolution into neighbouring countries, declared war on Austria on 20 April, 1792. And the king, whose only hope lay in foreign intervention, signed this declaration of war. Prussia joined Austria. On 11 July, the Assembly declared a state of national emergency.

The radical revolutionary clubs, the *Jacobins* and the *Cordeliers*, now prepared a new insurrection, led by violent men like Danton and Marat.

George Washington crossing the
Delaware river

The insurrection of 10 August was provoked by the Duke of Brunswick, commander of the Prussian and Austrian armies. In a manifesto he threatened to destroy Paris if the royal family were harmed and if his invading troops were not aided by the French people. The incensed mob lashed the manifesto to the gates of the Tuileries. A frenzied Paris mob broke into the royal palace. It was a massacre. Men were thrown out of windows, impaled, burned; there were nine hundred killed.

Louis fled to the Assembly for protection, but the latter suspended the king from office and imprisoned him at Luxembourg. Three days later, the *Commune*, presided over by Danton, imprisoned the royal family at the Temple. During the first days of September, hundreds of prisoners accused of plotting against the revolution were massacred in the prisons of Paris.

The Boston Tea Party

Meanwhile, enemy forces advanced on France. Danton declared: " Boldness, and again boldness, and always boldness and we shall save the fatherland! ". The French scored a victory over the Prussians at Valmy on 20 September, 1792.

At the same time, the Convention met, and almost their first act was to declare France a republic. The Convention then tried Louis XVI on a charge of betraying his country. He was found guilty and went to the guillotine on 21 January, 1793.

Scene from Goethe's
The sorrows of Young Werther

The idea of liberty was contagious, and France offered to assist all peoples willing to overthrow their governments. France entered the Rhineland and Belgium, but was repulsed. The Austrians invaded Flandres; the Prussians attacked Alsace. The English occupied Corsica and Toulon. Lazare Carnot, who was responsible for universal conscription, mobilised all the young French men, placing them under the command of young and brilliant generals: Hoche, Jourdan, Kléber and Marceau. The French army was now raised to over 700,000 men. A halt was put to the invasion of France by the end of 1793 and continuing French victories forced Prussia, Holland and Spain to make peace with France in 1795.

Immanuel Kant

The Convention adopted a democratic constitution in 1793, approving the

The Montgolfier balloon

Illustration showing a scene from *Faust*, Goethe's masterpiece. Mephistopheles is knocking at the door of Faust's home. Faust, the old disheartened poet, had made a pact with Mephistopheles, who promised him extraordinary experiences. Faust is the symbol of the insatiability of human knowledge and experience.

OPPOSITE PAGE, BOTTOM: Captain James Cook disembarking at the New Hebrides Islands, where he was amiably welcomed by the natives. Cook was the first person to sail across the Antarctic Circle; Tahiti was among the islands that he discovered.

RIGHT: George Washington, commander of the American forces during the War of Independence and first President of the United States of America. This portrait of Washington is by Charles Wilson Peale. The American War of Independence, 1775-1781, was preceded by about ten years of unrest and by rebellions of the colonists. England, weakened by the Seven Years' War, had raised taxes and refused representation to the colonies in the Parliament at London.

One of the most infamous episodes of the period was the Boston massacre, 5 March, 1770

ON THE OPPOSITE PAGE, TOP: The scene is depicted by Paul Revere, Metropolitan Museum of Art. The soldiers attacked the citizens who were protesting against the new fiscal system.

The storming of the Bastille

Goethe in Italy

The flight of Louis XVI

A rabid Republican

The Brandenburg Gate

decree of universal military conscription and fixing maximum prices to check inflation. Laws were enacted to permit the French peasant to become owners of the land they worked. A system of lower and higher education was introduced.

Unhappily, the highest spirit of the revolution degenerated during the Reign of Terror conducted by Robespierre. A terrible tribunal, presided over by Fouquier-Tinville, condemned to death hundreds of people, without them having the chance to defend themselves, and sent them to the guillotine. But this excess brought a reaction. It was the turn of Fouquier-Tinville and Robespierre to mount the scaffold on 28 July, 1794. A new Constitution was issued under which the *Directory* came into being. Corrupt and disorderly, this government by anarchy lasted only four years.

Meanwhile, the war against England and Austria continued. Napoleon Bonaparte, already a general, fought and defeated the Austrian army in three decisive battles in Italy. After these victories, Austria made peace at Campo Formio, on 17 October, 1797, under the terms of which France received Belgium and the Ionian Isles. Napoleon then decided to attack Britain's Indian empire through Egypt. But, after capturing Alexandria and defeating the Egyptian army at the Pyramids on 21 July, 1798, Napoleon's fleet was destroyed by Admiral Nelson at the Nile and his armies were cut off from France.

During this campaign, Napoleon learned that the powers of the Directory were diminishing. Seeing this as his chance to seize power, he hastily returned to France, where his popularity now was immense. By his *coup-d'état* on 9 November, he overthrew the Directory and established the Consulate, assuming practically all power to himself with the title First Consul.

In record time Napoleon transformed the administration of France. In 1801, he negotiated a Concordat with Pope Pius VII, which ended the confused relations between church and state caused by the French Revolution. He centralised the Government, facilitating administrative, legal and fiscal reforms. He also founded the Legion of Honour and put an end to the war

The battle of the Pyramids

Parisian fashion in 1795

Printing

General Bonaparte

The English occupying Malta

against Britain in 1802 with the Treaty of Amiens.

In 1804, Bonaparte crowned himself Napoleon I, Emperor of France. He bestowed peerages on some of his generals and his civil servants, but he gave them no privileges. He was the absolute ruler and those who dared oppose him were exiled. He introduced new cultures into France, such as making sugar from beetroot, excavating canals and making roads; but he also increased taxes. And, above all, he concentrated all his attention on his army.

It was intolerable to the English that the French should hold Antwerp: "a pistol aimed at England". War between France and England was renewed in 1803. During the next eleven years France fought Spain and all of Europe. There were resounding victories for Napoleon's forces at Austerlitz, Wagram, Jena, Friedland . . . they subdued Austria, Prussia, even Russia. But England held the seas: Nelson crushed the French fleet at Trafalgar in 1805.

By 1810, the French empire extended from the north of Germany to the Pyrénées, from the Atlantic ocean to Rome. It was a powerful empire, in which Napoleon's own brothers were kings of Holland, Naples and Spain.

Now Napoleon issued a decree inaugurating the Continental System—an attempt to defeat England by closing the ports of Europe to her trade. But, in 1811, the refusal of Russia to abide by the Continental System, as well as numerous other disputes between the two countries, caused Napoleon to invade Russia. He succeeded in occupying Moscow. But, in December, with the temperature at -37°C., the French forces were considerably reduced by cold and hunger and decimated by constant Russian attacks. Napoleon was forced to order the famous retreat.

Less than 100,000 men of the original 600,000 French force survived this disastrous Russian campaign. This loss in manpower, together with the accumulating impoverishment of the nation, was the beginning of the end for the great French empire.

On 31 March, 1814, the Allies occupied Paris. Napoleon abdicated and was sent into exile on the island of Elba. A brother of Louis XVI became king of France under the name of Louis XVIII.

Furniture in the style of Louis XVI.

A drawing-room, with furniture by Thomire and Carlin.

A dining-room; the silver soup tureen belonged to Catherine of Russia.

TOP: *The Tennis Court Oath*, a work by the French painter, Jacques Louis David. Representatives of the third estate, which consisted of 600 commoners, withdrew in dissatisfaction from the meeting of the States-General at Versailles. They held their own meeting in a nearby tennis court on 20 June, 1789, when they pledged that they would not disband until they had given France a new constitution. This was the prologue to the French Revolution.

ABOVE (LEFT TO RIGHT): The leaders of the Jacobins, members of the National Assembly: Robespierre, Marat, Danton and Saint-Just. After the fall of the Girondins, a moderate movement, the Jacobins instigated the terrors to which they themselves fell victim. This was the most tragic period of the Revolution.

RIGHT: The execution of Louis XVI, on 21 January, 1793. Louis and his family tried to flee France, but were arrested. Louis was tried and found guilty of treason.

William Tell, **by Schiller**

Robert Fulton's *Clermont*,
the first successful steamboat

**Alexander Humboldt
in South America**

Nelson at Trafalgar

Fashion in 1805

Conditions in France seemed to be taking a backward step, with the returned political exiles seeking to revive their ancient privileges. The French people would not support these arrogant men who had " learned nothing and forgotten nothing ". Induced by news of this unrest to try to recover his lost throne, Napoleon left Elba, landed in France on 1 March, 1815, and marched towards Paris, where he was welcomed enthusiastically by the army and the people. Louis XVIII fled to Belgium. In vain, Napoleon declared that he wanted only peace. The Allies united in battle against him and he was finally defeated at Waterloo on 18 June, 1815, by the combined armies of Great Britain, Prussia, Austria and Russia, commanded by the Duke of Wellington, only a short Hundred Days after his arrival in Paris. Napoleon abdicated again and was taken to the island of St. Helena where he was kept, under strong British guard, until his death in 1821.

The Allies met at the Congress of Vienna to refashion the map of Europe. Most of Poland was given to Russia. Prussia received territories on the Rhine and Austria received Lombardy and Venetia. Britain retained Malta, Heligoland, Ceylon, Cape Colony and certain West Indian islands, thereby holding her position as the leading colonial empire, with supremacy on all the seas of the world. Britain ruled supreme. Having fended off French rivalry, she was queen of the world.

The European rulers, having disposed of Napoleon, now united in the Holy Alliance. Proposed by Tsar Alexander I, its declared purpose was to unite the rulers of Europe to advance Christian principles. It was, in fact, only an optimistic statement of the Christian brotherhood of rulers, but it was regarded by liberals as a sinister conspiracy among autocratic monarchs to suppress all liberal democratic movements. England was not a party to this alliance: commerce was of more concern to her than vague idealistic theories. In 1818, when the occupation forces had left France, who had by then paid her war debts, Louis XVIII was admitted, on equal footing, to the circle of rulers.

But already the people were in revolt. The treaties of 1815 had created

The Allies crossing the Rhine

Execution of Spanish guerrillas

The telephone of Sömmering

revolutionary situations: Polish Catholics were placed under a Protestant king of Prussia and an Orthodox Tsar; Finland was under the protection of the Russians; the Italians were governed by the Hapsburgs. Under these conditions it was inevitable that a spirit of nationalism should arise. Revolts broke out in Italy and in Spain, where Louis XVIII sent an army to return Ferdinand VII to his throne in the name of the Holy Alliance. The French troops scored an easy victory at Trocadero, near Cadiz. But it was only a very temporary victory: the aspirations of nationalism were to produce wars and revolutions for the whole of the century.

Latin America was the first to shake off the yoke of Madrid and Lisbon. Insurrections occurred in Mexico, Colombia and Peru, promoted by the British, who were anxious to open these countries to trading. The most celebrated hero of these wars of independence was Bolivar the Liberator, who gave his name to one of these countries, Bolivia. In 1830, Latin America was broken up into six states which were torn asunder by civil war. Only Brazil, which had broken away from Portugal and elected Pedro, son of John VI, as its emperor, enjoyed a comparative peace.

The fire of Moscow

In Europe, trouble broke out when the people of Paris rose up against Charles X, who succeeded his brother, Louis XVIII, in 1824. Charles had become increasingly unpopular among the middle class, because he granted compensation to the *émigrés* for their lands confiscated during the Revolution. He abdicated and fled to England and the Duke of Orléans was proclaimed king, under the title of Louis Philippe.
On 4 October, the Belgians, aided by the French and the English, revolted against the crown of Holland and proclaimed the independence of Belgium.

Then Poland tried to overthrow the Russian domination. They hoped for the support of France, but Louis Philippe did not come to their rescue and, on 7 September, 1831, the Polish revolution was crushed by the Russian army.

The bicycle of Drais

Italy also rose up against the Pope and against Austria, who quelled these

On 2 December, 1804, Napoleon was consecrated Emperor of France at Notre Dame Cathedral in Paris. This painting, which hangs in the Louvre, is by the French artist Jacques Louis David. At the moment when Pope Pius VII lifted the crown to place it on Napoleon's head, Napoleon took it from him and crowned himself; then he also crowned his wife, Josephine. The significance of this gesture was evident: Napoleon would not submit to the Papal authority. Nevertheless, it is to Napoleon's credit that he brought religious peace to France by signing the Concordat which regularised the status of the Catholic Church in France.

BELOW, OPPOSITE PAGE: Napoleon's army, commanded by the King of Naples, Murat, enters Moscow. The city is deserted, the Russians abandoned it after having set it on fire. Deprived of reinforcements, the French began, a few days later, the tragic retreat during which they lost three hundred and fifty thousand soldiers, victims of cold and starvation. This disaster marked the end of the glorious reign of Napoleon, who was beaten the following year at Leipzig by the allied armies of Prussia, Russia, Sweden and Austria.

TOP, RIGHT: The last letter written by Nelson to Lady Hamilton, shortly before the Battle of Trafalgar. The letter reads: "*The last lines I am writing before the battle are to you and I trust I shall survive to finish this letter.*" But, on the bridge of the *Victory*, the victorious admiral met with his death.

Victory Octr: 19th 1805
Noon Cadiz ESE 16 Leagues

125

My Dearest beloved Emma the dear
friend of my bosom the Signal has
been made that the Enemys Combined
fleet are coming out of Port, We
have very little Wind so that I have
no hopes of seeing them before to morrow
May the God of Battles crown my
Endeavours with success at all events
I will take care that my name shall ever
be most dear to you and Horatia both
of whom I love as much as my own
life, and as my last writing before the
battle will be to you so I hope in God that
I shall live to finish my letter after the

The Congress of Vienna

Empire-style furniture

The Battle of Waterloo

A miner's lamp

The *Savannah*

insurrections. In Germany, the more moderate liberals obtained, in certain states, their own constitutional government.

The years between the revolutions of 1830 and 1848 were characterised by upheavals of quite a different order: the first Industrial Revolution began in England, France, the Rhineland and the United States.
Farming methods had not changed over the centuries until, in 1828, Patrick Bell invented a harvester; then came threshers, mechanical sowers and ploughs. The Americans, who had vast virgin territories to cultivate, were the first to adopt these machines.
Coal was needed to operate the steam engine invented by James Watt and England had rich coalfields. In 1829, England was using almost fifteen thousand steam engines; France had three thousand. The textile industry was the first to benefit from Watt's invention; this industry developed rapidly.
To enable him to make up material into soldiers' uniforms more quickly, a little French provincial tailor named Barthélemy Thimonnier invented the first practical sewing machine in 1829; it could sew two hundred stitches a minute. The idea was perfected by a Boston tailor named Elias Howe who, in 1852, opened a factory to make sewing machines. A similar enterprise was started two years later by another American, Singer, whose machines are still sold all over the world.
A Scot named MacIntosh, using rubber imported from Brazil, made a waterproof material from which the first raincoats were produced. One can understand why this invention originated in Scotland, which has over thirteen inches of rainfall a year, six times more than London or Brest.
The first steam boat was American; it was called the *Savannah*. But it also used sails on its twenty-five day voyage from New York to Liverpool. The public were wary of these new inventions. When, in 1838, a British steamship capable of carrying one hundred and eleven passengers left Bristol for New York, there were only seven travellers on board.

On land, people travelled about in stage coaches, huge carriages drawn by five horses, which achieved speeds of three or four miles an hour. Then vehicles powered by steam were produced in England which could reach over fifteen miles an hour. The stage coach owners, seeing the danger of such competition, obtained a ruling from the government which obliged all

Napoleon at Saint Helena

The independence of Liberia

Simon Bolivar

Lord Byron in Greece

Fashion in 1825

steam vehicles to be preceded, on foot or horseback, by a man bearing a red flag. This was to safeguard the population from this new menace on the public roads. George Stephenson was then perfecting his famous steam locomotive, the *Rocket* (1829), which travelled at the then fantastic speed of 30 m.p.h. This, too, received a wary reception from the public. It was claimed that the smoke would kill vegetation and choke the birds, that the flying sparks would set fire to crops and houses, and that the travellers would perish in the dark tunnels.

A member of Parliament asked Stephenson: "And what will happen, Mr. Stephenson, if a cow is lying on the track?" "That will be too bad for the cow," replied Stephenson.

Despite all opposition, the railroads multiplied.

They were particularly useful across the great sweep of the United States; by 1850 there were already 8,942 miles of railroad.

We owe the invention of the dynamo and the great electricity systems of today to Argo, Ampère and Faraday. Samuel Morse, an American portrait painter, invented the first successful electric telegraph and the Morse code: a system of dots, dashes and spaces that telegraphists can use to send messages by wire. Alfred Vail helped Morse in the development of the telegraph. In France, in 1829, Louis Daguerre invented, in collaboration with Joseph Niepce, a process of recording images on metal plates, called *daguerreotypes*. The industrial Revolution naturally brought about a concentration of capital. London became the great financial centre of the world, where enormous fortunes were built up. Unfortunately, these fortunes were amassed at the expense of the miserable workers, who were crowded together in the over-populated towns. Foul slums disgraced the great industrial cities of England and France. Men worked up to eighteen hours a day for starvation wages. Six-year-old children worked down the English mines, harnessed to the coal trucks; they cost less than horses.

Writers like Carlyle and Dickens in England and Victor Hugo in France denounced the scandal. But it was not without lively opposition that the English Parliament passed laws forbidding the employment of children of less than nine years, and also limiting their working hours to thirteen, then to ten hours, in 1847. These abominations were not aired in the great newspapers which were born in this mechanised age: these newspapers thrived on advertising from the employers.

But the sociologists questioned and sought answers: Robert Owen in

ABOVE, LEFT TO RIGHT: The main founders of the Holy Alliance: Tsar Alexander I of Russia; Francis I, Emperor of Austria, and King Frederick William III of Prussia.

LEFT: The throne room in the ducal palace at Parma. The Duke of Parma put it at the disposal of Marie-Louise of Austria, daughter of Francis I and second wife of Napoleon, for the Congress of Vienna.

RIGHT: This room, furnished in the Empire style, contains Napoleon's bed from the Palace of Bordeaux. Among the Empire-style motifs, besides the imperial bees and the 'N', one can see the Greek-Roman motifs —chimeras, winged victories, eagles, swords— and the Egyptian motifs —sphinx, beetles, head of Isis.

William Blake and Francisco Goya were artists who, at the beginning of the 19th century, broke away from the classical tradition in order to create original work.

RIGHT: the *Creation of Adam*, a Bible illustration by the poet and painter Blake; BELOW: *The Giant*, by Goya.

BELOW, RIGHT: Friedrich Schiller, romantic dramatist, and Ludwig van Beethoven, German musician of genius.

The first contest between locomotives at Rainhill

The Polish revolt of 1831

The discovery of the magnetic pole

Breech-loading gun

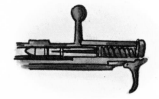

England; Fourier, August Comte and Proudhon in France. Gradually, the idea of socialism was born, resulting in the publication, in 1848, of the Communist Manifesto, an exposition of the views of Karl Marx and Friedrich Engels on the class struggle.

Even the poets rejected the world in which they lived, but middle-class platitudes inspired them more than the misery of the people. Lord Byron created the model of the romantic hero, the idol of the young, who scorned society, in particular, and humanity, in general, as unworthy of the purity of his soul. Each one beat his breast in anguish, that was the spirit of the age: Chateaubriand, Vigny, Musset, Shelley, Keats, Wordsworth.

Romanticism expressed itself in paintings by Delacroix, Lawrence, Turner. But the greatest painter of his time, Goya, combined a romantic passion with a cruel realism. Similarly in music, Beethoven, the greatest of them all, aired his passion in the classical forms, opening the way to Schubert, Schumann and Chopin.

In 1846, an economic crisis, caused mainly by a very bad harvest, swept over western Europe. To relieve its starving, England decided to repeal the Corn Law, which taxed the importation of wheat, introducing instead a system of free trade. England, the first industrial, maritime, financial and colonial power, had no fear of competition. India remained for her always a marvellous source of riches, from which she could watch over her bases in Egypt, Aden and Singapore. In Hong-Kong, British merchants were opening up the immense Chinese market. And a thousand poor people who daily left England were settling in Canada, British Colombia, New Zealand and Australia.

But this is how the economic crisis, allied to the new spirit of liberalism and nationalism, affected Europe. Paris—" the crater of revolutions " as Victor Hugo described it—went into eruption. The people demanded electoral reform. This degenerated into a riot, during which Louis Philippe fled to England. France proclaimed a republic on 25 February, 1848. When this was announced the liberals of the princely states of southern Germany demanded a constitution and the union of the German states. The people of Milan, Venice and Hungary proclaimed their independence from Austria. The Czechs demanded self-government from Vienna and also claimed the kingdom of Bohemia. The armies of Austria, Russia and Prussia intervened harshly to quell these revolts.

The great revolutionary movement began in France, where disagreements

The laboratory of Justus von Liebig

The conversion of magnetic current

The Morse telegraph

Queen Victoria

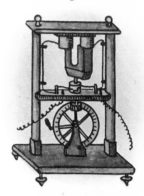

Photographic equipment of
Louis Daguerre

about reforms and the struggle between the working people and the middle class marked the beginning of a new class struggle and the rise of socialism as an important political philosophy. In June, the French army defeated rioting workers in a street battle in Paris.

The glory of machinery was shown for the first time in London at the exhibition of 1851, where all the nations displayed their industrial and scientific inventions.

The Second Republic elected as its president Louis Napoleon, nephew of Napoleon Bonaparte. He became emperor in 1852, launching the Second Empire. Napoleon was aware of the problems brought on by the Industrial Revolution. He favoured state aid for industry, banks and railways, and state action to end poverty. He tried to alleviate the misery of the workers by increasing the social amenities: hospitals, nurseries and alms houses. Napoleon was one of the first statesmen to propose general disarmament and he tried to settle disputes between countries through international conferences. In 1849, he helped to overthrow the Roman Republic and to restore the Pope and, in 1863, he unsuccessfully tried to help the Polish people in their revolt against Russia.

The United States had greatly enlarged their territory and their population had grown from six million people to twenty-five million. France had sold them Louisiana in 1803; Spain had given them Florida in 1819; they had taken Texas, New Mexico and California from Mexico, in 1848: an area equal to Germany, France and Spain together.

At the end of 1840, immigrants were arriving from all over Europe. When they could find no work for themselves in the eastern towns they broke into the virgin lands of the west. They travelled in tarpaulin-covered wagons, into which were crammed the women and children, luggage, tools and provisions. The men followed the wagons on foot or on horseback. Inexorably, the frontiers moved west, driving back the Indians and their bisons. As soon as the United States had annexed California, gold was discovered there. Immediately there was a gold rush, in which some people made immense fortunes in a matter of months.

But this great democracy of free enterprise continued to tolerate the slavery which was rife in the southern states. The stage was being set for a mighty clash.

LEFT: Alessandro Manzoni, novelist, poet and dramatist, one of the greatest figures of Italian literature. The first edition of his masterpiece, *The Betrothed Lovers*, appeared in 1827.

OPPOSITE PAGE: The Battle of Navarin, painted by the contemporary artist, Thomas Lang. After the defeat of the Turkish fleet by the English, Greece obtained independence.

The Congress of Vienna, which tried to arrange frontiers and create governments without taking account of the stirrings of nationalism and the feeling of small Powers, gave rise to numerous revolts. After Greece had gained her independence, France freed herself of the Bourbon monarchy. In 1831, Belgium broke away from Holland to which she had been arbitrarily united by the creation of the kingdom of the Netherlands.

LEFT: Louis Philippe, the first constitutional king, presents himself to the French people.

ABOVE: Leopold I, king of the Belgians.

Construction of an iron ship

The Last of the Mohicans

Edgar Allan Poe

The phantom ship

The first telegraph line

Russia endured a mild form of slavery, serfdom. The peasants were grouped in communities, *mirs*, under the government of *starostes*, who combined the duties of village mayors and bailiffs of the noblemen. These peasants neither knew how to read nor write.

Nicholas I mistrusted the liberal ideas of western Europe. While effecting industrial improvements—by having canals built and by undertaking the construction of a first railway—he forbade teachers and students to go abroad without authorisation. In 1849, he went so far as to condemn to death twenty-one students for having read foreign books. Their sentences were commuted to hard labour in Siberia. One of these students was to be one of the greatest Russian writers: Dostoyevsky.

Alexander II, who came to the throne in 1855, freed the serfs of the crown and, in 1861, an *ukase* (decree) extended the reform to the whole of Russia and provided for plots of land to be paid for over a period of forty-nine years. The serfs were not altogether appreciative of this decree. They were to pay in instalments, certainly, but ultimately they were paying for land which they considered theirs by inheritance. The paradoxical result of this liberal measure was that many of the peasants emigrated towards the east, towards Siberia, where they hoped to find lands to cultivate, and thus the nobility suffered by the decree.

China was in the throes of one of her customary crises. Over-population, drought, plagues of locusts and catastrophic floods led to a revolt of giant proportions. The Tai-ping rebellion seized Nanking, marched on Peking, and reached Tientsin in 1853. The Europeans took advantage of these events and entered Peking and obtained from the emperor the control of the maritime customs. Then they helped the Manchu dynasty to suppress the Tai-ping rebellion. While they were there, the French occupied Cochin China and imposed their protectorate in Cambodia (1863).

The Americans became more and more impassioned by the question of slavery. Abraham Lincoln, whose father was a poor pioneer, revealed a great eloquence in debates on the matter and succeeded, in 1858, in being nominated by the Republicans for the United States Senate. " This government ", he said, " cannot endure permanently, half slave and half free ". On 6 November, 1860, he became President of the United States. On 4 February, 1861, the seven states of the kingdom of cotton and of slavery South Carolina, Georgia, Alabama, Florida, Mississippi, Louisiana and Texas united themselves into the Confederate States of America, adopted their own Constitution and elected a president, Jefferson Davis. On 4 March,

A town in North America

Karl Marx

The February Revolution

German Parliament

Pedal bicycle

the day of his inauguration, Lincoln solemnly swore to uphold, protect and defend the Constitution of the United States. The Confederate replied by opening fire on a federal fortress, Fort Sumter, on 12 April.

On 15 April, the President called all the citizens to the defence of the Union. It was the beginning of a fratricidal war, the War of Secession, which was to last four years.
The Southern generals, Lee and Jackson, defied with impunity the Northerners and won a decisive victory over them on 4 May, 1863, at Chancellorsville.
General Lee followed up this victory by moving towards the north of Washington. He met the federal armies on 1 July at Gettysburg. For three days a formidable battle raged, killing 20,000. The Southerners were forced to retreat, but it took another two years to curtail their activities completely. Profiting from the state of war, Lincoln passed an amendment to the Constitution: the abolition of slavery. It was only on 9 April, 1865, that General Lee surrendered to General Grant. The civil war had cost the Northerners 360,000 lives, and the Southerners 260,000. The Union had been preserved, but it was still uncertain whether all Americans, black or white, were to be free. Lincoln, who wanted to reconcile the North and South, was assassinated by a fanatic on 14 April, 1865. The South was given up to demagogy and anarchy.
The War of Secession had seemed to Napoleon III a good opportunity to set foot in America. Mexico was, as always, in a state of revolution. Juárez, president of the liberals, having conquered the government, had suspended the payment of interest on debts contracted in the west and particularly in France. France, England and Spain sent contingents to Mexico. After a year England and Spain withdrew, but Napoleon III reinforced his troops, who entered Mexico City, where they proclaimed Maximilian, brother of the emperor of Austria, Emperor of Mexico (1864). Three years later, in 1867, Napoleon was forced to withdraw his army because of pressure from the United States. Juárez seized Maximilian and had him executed.
France's thoughts already lay elsewhere. Bismarck, Chancellor of Prussia, had undertaken to unify Germany under the authority of Prussia. First he had to eliminate Austria, which he did without difficulty by the victory of Sadowa, 3 July, 1866. Prussia expanded from the Russian frontier to the French frontier, but still many states remained outside of her power. Bismarck declared, " The nation can only be tightly united in a communal anger ".

OPPOSITE PAGE, LEFT: **Three eminent people from the first half of the 19th century.** TOP TO BOTTOM: **Heinrich Heine, François-René de Chateaubriand, Honoré de Balzac.**

RIGHT: **The glass pavilion built by Joseph Paxton for Albert, Prince Consort, husband of Queen Victoria, on the occasion of the first world exposition which took place in London in 1851. Three hundred thousand square yards of glass and 44 miles of iron bars were used in its construction.**

ABOVE: **Guiseppe Mazzini, in exile in London, teaching needy Italian children. The proud Genoese republican was the political educator of the Italians. The designs of the Young Italy, his secret society, were clear: unity, republic, independence. In order to attain his ends he did not rely on the support of foreign powers but on the people. This party failed as much through misfortune as through the excessive temerity of its partisans.**

OPPOSITE PAGE, BOTTOM: **Two men watching the moon, a picture by Kasper David Friedrich, master of romantic Dutch painting. (Dresden Gallery).**

The Suez Canal

Joseph Garibaldi

Philipp Reis' telephone

Louis Pasteur

Selling of slaves in the
Southern States of America

This anger was indeed capable of incensing him when the time came.
In 1867, Paris in turn celebrated the marvels of industry in a world exhibition at Champ-de-Mars. It was visited by fifteen million people, amongst whom about fifteen were monarchs. Paris was illuminated by gas lights and presented a completely new face, a step in front of the modern cities, with her spacious thoroughfares and squares.

During 1867, an event of great import took place in Japan. For nearly seven hundred years the *shoguns*, the great feudal lords, had governed the country in the name of the emperor. But when their feudal vassals, the *daimios*, rebelled, the young emperor, Mutsuhito, announced that he intended " to alone exert the supreme power over interior and exterior affairs ". He left Kyoto, where he had been residing under supervision, and transferred his capital to Yedo, which he named Tokyo, " capital of the East ". Japan entered the era of enlightenment: it was to westernise itself with incredible rapidity.
Spain, where civil wars alternated with military insurrections, offered Bismark, in 1870, the opportunity for which he had been waiting—to fight France. General Prim, who had just expelled Queen Isabella II, was looking for a king. He offered the crown to Prince Léopold of Hohenzollern-Sigmaringen. Bismarck persuaded him to accept. When the news broke out, France was incensed: she did not wish to see a Germanic prince on the throne of Charles V. William I, of Prussia, who was opposed to the enterprise, begged Leopold to refuse the Spanish crown. The incident seemed resolved; Bismarck had been defeated.
But new demands by the extremist French party, excited by Bismarck, led France to declare war on Prussia on 17 July, 1870. September 2 saw the disaster of Sedan. On 4 September, the legislative body voted the deposition of Napoleon III; Gambetta and Jules Favre declared the republic. Paris, besieged, surrendered on 28 January, 1871. By the Treaty of Frankfort, 10 May, France found itself forced to give up Alsace and the northern part of Lorraine (except for the region of Belfort) and to pay a war indemnity of £200 million; an army of occupation was to remain in the north and in the east until payment of this indemnity.
The French had elected a National Constituent Assembly, which met at Bordeaux on 12 February and nominated Thiers ' head of executive power of the French Republic '. Then it moved to Versailles. The Parisians, overwhelmed by defeat, unemployment and poverty, lived in a state of

The first prospectors for petroleum in the United States

Execution of Maximilian, Emperor of Mexico

Transcontinental railway in the United States

The Red Cross

Mendel's theory

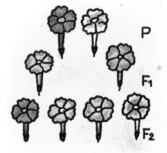

uneasiness. On 3 March, a group of republicans seized two hundred cannons which had been assembled in Montmartre. Thiers ordered their recovery, the soldiers refused to obey. The insurrection took the aspect of a proletarian revolution which elected a Communal Council, soon to be called the Commune of Paris, which adopted the red flag. Thiers had left Paris in the hands of the rebels, he now undertook to retake the capital by force. The affair lasted two months. On 21 May, the 'Bloody Week' began, which brought down the Communards. District by district, Paris burned. On 28 May, when the last of the soldiers of the Commune had been shot against the wall of the Père-Lachaise cemetery, the repression had cost 20,000 lives.

England had no other anxiety but to enlarge and arrange her colonial empire. In India, she built roads and railways, developed the cultivation of rice, corn, cotton and tea. She employed the natives in the subaltern administrative posts. In 1877, Prime Minister Disraeli, champion of imperialism, proclaimed Queen Victoria as Empress of the Indies in Delhi.

In the countries of English population, London steered a liberal course. Canada became an independent state in 1871, united to England by the Crown. Gold was discovered in Australia in 1851. Ten years later, 275,000 English were installed there, enjoying an exceptionally high standard of living for that time. Workers there were the first to obtain a forty-eight hour working week. In 1872, the colony of Cape Town received a statute of self-government. The Suez Canal, constructed by Ferdinand de Lesseps, and opened in 1869, enabled the first voyage from London to Bombay in eighteen days. A time which made it possible for Philéas Fogg, in 1872, to make his trip round the world in eighty days.

Joint-stock companies multiplied at the same time as their sizes increased. Owing to their considerable profits, they were able to invest their capital throughout the world. All the railways which were constructed then were financed by western funds, with the sole exception of those in the United States. Coal was the all-important force behind this activity and Great Britain yielded half the world tonnage.

Technology brought daily advancements. Locomotives could travel at 70 m.p.h., France produced a new, extremely light metal called aluminium, which was discovered in 1854. The rotary printing press first installed by *The Times* in London, speeded up newspaper production. In 1873, Remington invented his first typewriter. In the United States the first paraffin refinery was opened. In 1863, paraffin was used to power an extraordinary new

ABOVE: **The Battle of Seven Days—portrayed in a lithograph of the time—in the course of which the Northerner, General McClellan, sought in vain to seize Richmond, capital of the Southerners, held by the forces of General Lee. This was an important event in the American Civil War.**

BELOW: **Florence Nightingale, the famous English nurse. At the hospital in Scutari, on the Bosphorus, during the Crimean War, the courageous young girl, with the help of thirty-eight companions, organised the first proper, effective health service for the care of wounded soldiers.**

Richard Wagner and his music. A caricature of the time clearly shows the strong personality of the artist.

Camillo Benso, Count di Cavour, the very able Italian statesman who helped to bring about the unification of Italy.

BELOW: gold diggers in California. (Lithograph from the Library of Congress, Washington).

Stanley meeting Livingstone

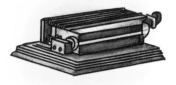

Siemens' dynamo

Bismarck

Robert Koch

Alexander Bell's telephone

machine: the motor car. The first motor race, Paris-Rouen, took place on 7 November, 1869. The average speed was just over 7 m.p.h., French, German, Italian and Belgian researchers worked on the question of the practical applications of electricity. In 1877, came the telephone and, in 1896, the wireless. In 1854, an American capitalist, Field, had the ambitious idea of linking America and Europe by a 2,480 mile submarine cable: the venture lasted nine years.

The electrical exhibition in Paris, in 1881, offered to the public the latest inventions which were to transform the daily life of man.

With electric light he could go to bed later, rise earlier. The lift spared him the trouble of having to climb the stairs. The internal combustion engine allowed him the thrill of speed without breaking his back, thanks to the veterinary surgeon, Dunlop, who developed the first pneumatic tyre, and to the Michelin brothers who improved upon his invention. In 1888, Eastman launched the Kodak.

Scientific discoveries succeeded one another, in physics as well as in chemistry and astronomy. None more useful to humanity than those of Louis Pasteur (vaccine against rabies), of Koch (discovery of the germ causing tuberculosis), and of Jenner (vaccine against smallpox).

The Constitution of 1875 gave France a president of the Republic and two assemblies, the Senate and the Chamber of Deputies. Jules Ferry, Minister of Public Education, instituted free and undenominational primary education. The great western powers opened the markets of Africa and Asia. France and England had become the dominant powers in Africa. Bismarck rejoiced, confident that sooner or later they would find themselves in conflict. In 1881, Tunisia was occupied by the French. The English occupied Egypt, having eliminated the French. The two countries were in equal competition for Madagascar, which finally became a French colony in 1896. During that year, Italy, who sought to take possession of Ethiopia, suffered a disastrous defeat at Adowa.

The English made a general movement of expansion from Cairo in the north and from the colony of the Cape in the south. The French set out from western Africa. It was inevitable that their paths should cross. The meeting took place when an English column, moving up the Nile with 20,000 men, met Captain Marchand with 200 men from Gabon. Marchand, who was the first to arrive at Fashoda, refused to surrender. In the last days of October, 1898, war seemed inevitable. But France, already torn asunder by the

A street scene in 1885

Edison's phonograph

Dreyfus affair and, moreover, incapable of competing on the sea with England, surrendered.

Why should France and England make war ? They had the whole planet to exploit. But Germany, created by Bismarck, reigned over central and western Europe.

In order to withstand Germany and Italy, the French could see only one solution: the Russian Alliance, signed in 1893. Russia had made some progress in the social sphere. Since Alexander II had abolished serfdom, in 1858, the autocracy had been somewhat relaxed, and the Intelligentsia had awoken. Under the reign of Nicholas II, the last of the tsars, who came to the throne in 1894, Russia, like Japan, was in the process of passing from the Middle Ages to the industrial era. But great troubles shook the country. The *moujiks* lived in poverty, crowded in their wooden isbas, underfed, diseased and illiterate. Gogol, Gorky, Tolstoy, Chekhov, Dostoyevsky, in their works, have left us powerful descriptions. The Russian people were ripe for a revolution, but nobody could foretell what form it would take.

In 1894, the Japanese conquered Korea, penetrated Manchuria, opened the route to Peking, and forced China to sign, in 1895, a treaty by which the latter was to surrender Formosa and Port Arthur, and abandon the suzerainty of Korea. China called upon the aid of European financiers, to whom she granted territories and commercial benefits in payment.

In Germany, William II proclaimed, " The German race is the salt of the earth ". The governor of the Indies, Houston Stewart, declared, " The British empire is, after Providence, the greatest auspicious force in the world ". Every nation believed itself to be the chosen nation. But out of this chauvinism was born racialism, and out of racialism, anti-Semitism.

It was France who had the unfortunate privilege of representing this movement with the Dreyfus affair. Captain Dreyfus, a Jew, was tried for treason in 1894. It was not until twelve years later that his innocence was recognised: twelve years during which France was torn between the partisans of justice and the partisans of the honour of the army.

About 1900, the kings of petrol, steel, aluminium, tin, electricity, and railways in the United States, had created all-powerful trusts. In this country of multi-millionaires, the workers were less unfortunate than elsewhere. They led a far more comfortable life than their counterparts in Europe, their work was better organised, and each one had the hope of becoming one of these multi-millionaires himself.

The Americans had no need to favour colonialism for they possessed an extensive market. However, they coveted the island of Cuba, which belonged to the

The first electric light

The English occupying Egypt

Heinrich Hertz

173

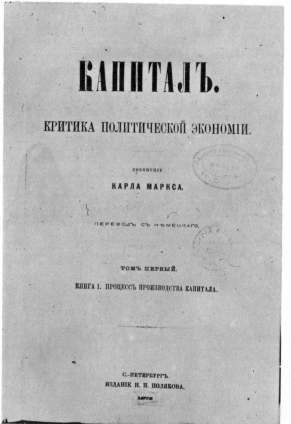

ABOVE: " Impression, rising sun " by Claude Monet from the Marmottan Museum, Paris. The title of this famous painting, exhibited in Paris in 1874, originated the name of Impressionism given to the new school of modern art.

LEFT: The first Russian translation of *Capital* appeared in 1872. *Das Capital*, recognised as the Bible of socialists, was the work of Karl Marx and Friedrich Engels, who finished it after the death of his master. It did not make a great impression on the liberal Russians, and the idea of abolishing private ownership did not gain popular favour. The revolution of 1917 did not have a Marxist movement at its root but started as a revolt against the absolute power of the tsars. The spirit of this revolt was similar to that which had presided at the liberal insurrections of other European states but, later on, a small group of convinced communists made use of it to conquer the power of the tsars.

174

In the 19th century, at the same time as the revolutionary disorders, the misery of the peasants and the ferment of new ideas, Russia saw a surprising efflorescence of artists, some of whom are represented here. ABOVE: Peter Tchaikovsky, one of the great Russian composers.

BELOW: Fyodor Dostoyevsky, the tormented genius who created *The Brothers Karamazov.*

Leo Tolstoy, author of *War and Peace* (ABOVE), and Nicholas Rimsky-Korsakov (BELOW), who found his inspiration in the tunes of Russian folklore.

The *Fram* in the icefields of the North Pole

Clément Ader's aeroplane *Éole*

Otto Lilienthal

The Lumière brothers

Revival of the Olympic Games

Spaniards, because it was the largest producer of sugar cane. They alleged humanitarian reasons—reproaching the Spaniards for repressing too strictly the revolts which had broken out in Cuba—for making war on Spain. In 1898, America declared Cuba and Porto Rico to be independent states, and annexed for itself the Philippines and the Hawaiian islands, where a naval base was installed which was to become the famous Pearl Harbour. Spain had lost the vestiges of her colonial empire.

The Spanish-American War had revealed the necessity of being able to move the United States' navy from one ocean to the other. This demonstrated the urgency to open a canal, the Panama Canal, for which the project, conceived by the Frenchman, Ferdinand de Lesseps, already existed. The Americans provoked a revolution in Colombia in 1902. A small 'independent' state, Panama, was created, which conceded to the United States the necessary territory to construct the canal.

At this time the world was enthusiastic about a war in South Africa where the English, led by Cecil Rhodes, were opposing the Dutch colonists, known as the *Boers*, who were settled in the Republic of the Transvaal and Orange Free State, led by an energetic man, Paul Kruger. The essence of the question was that Cecil Rhodes wanted to appropriate the gold mines of the Transvaal and gain the economic aid of the Boers for Cape Colony, where he was Prime Minister. To everybody's surprise, the Boers resisted for two and a half years, and compelled England to send 450,000 men against her. Finally, the victorious English offered the Boers an honourable peace by which they were to participate in the government of South Africa. They did this so well, in fact, that a few years later their leader, General Botha, was at the head of the government.

Another colonial war flared up in China. The old Empress T'seu-hi, supporting the agitators, the *Boxers*, brought about a massacre of Europeans in Peking. An international army comprising of English, Germans, Americans, French, Russians and Japanese intervened. The army occupied Peking and imposed great penalties on China.

In Korea and Manchuria, the Russians and the Japanese were facing each other in war. The Japanese were cramped for room on their small islands and they wanted to gain some land from Russia.

In January, 1902, Japan signed a military alliance treaty with England. The English tried to avoid a war with Russia, but when Japan made a proposition to Russia—Korea for herself and Manchuria for the Russians—Saint Peters-

First flight of the Wright brothers

Sven Hedin in central Asia

A Zeppelin

Albert Einstein

Naval battle of Tsushima

burg refused. On the night of the 8 and 9 February, 1904, the Japanese blew up the Russian fleet in the harbour of Port Arthur. The war then developed on land in Manchuria, where the Russians were routed. They later suffered a naval disaster at the battle of Tsu-shima.

These Japanese victories awoke great hopes in the Far East, and gave an impetus there to the nationalist movements.

On the 9 January, 1905, eight days after the Russian surrender at Port Arthur, the Russian people revolted in Saint Petersburg. The Cossacks charged them and the infantrymen fired without any regard for the numbers they killed. Nine hundred people were killed and five thousand wounded.

The next day a strike erupted in Moscow. To calm the troubles the tsar promised a Constitution, but he only instituted an advisory assembly, in August, 1905. The strike spread throughout Russia. Then, in the October Manifesto, Nicholas II granted the fundamental liberties and convoked the *Douma*, or elected assembly, who were to institute laws. This was the end of the absolute monarchy.

England, apprehensive of Germany's power, turned towards France. King Edward VII initiated a reconciliation when he went to Paris in 1903. The President of the French Republic, Émile Loubet, also visited him. These exchanges of friendship came to an end after the agreements of 8 April, 1904, which settled the colonial differences. This was not a political treaty, nor a military alliance, but an *entente cordiale* which assured France of the support of an Empire and gave England a fighting power on the Continent.

Germany was still attempting to secure her maritime and worldwide power. Wishing to destroy the Franco-English entente, she provoked incidents against the French, in Tangier in 1905 and in Agadir in 1911, but succeeded only in bringing England and France closer together. On the 4 November, 1911, a treaty was signed by which, in exchange for her freedom in Morocco, France ceded part of the French Congo to Germany.

About this time China at last rid herself of her old imperial finery. Sun Yat-sen, doctor of medicine at the English faculty of Hong Kong, who had resided in the United States and in England and who was converted to Protestantism and Marxism, founded a National People's Party in 1900, the Koumintang, whose members were recruited from among the intellectuals and merchants of the Canton region.

In 1911, the Chinese revolution began in the south.

The minister Yüan Shih-K'ai, in Peking, and Sun Yat-sen, in Nanking each

BELOW: Henry Ford photographed on a motorised quadricycle in 1904. Ford at once realised the importance of this new means of transport and was the first man to think of mass production, which made possible the sale of cars to the general public. After many attempts, he succeeded in manufacturing reasonably priced cars, which met with immediate success.

ABOVE, LEFT: Attack on the fortress of Port Arthur by the Japanese during the Chinese-Japanese Wars of 1894. The war was provoked by the expansionist policy of Japan, who wished to conquer Korea, where China asserted itself. The war ended with a thundering victory for the Japanese.

ABOVE, RIGHT: Pierre and Marie Curie who, in 1903, received the Nobel prize for physics. They discovered radium and polonium by isolating them from pitchblende (uranium ore).

BELOW: A demonstration by suffragettes in the streets of London. The Women's Social and Political Union, founded by Mrs. Emmeline Pankhurst and her daughter Christabel, took militant action to gain voting rights for women, and succeeded in doing so, for women over thirty, in 1918.

The sinking of the *Titanic*

Peary at the North Pole

A racing car of 1911

Demonstration of Chinese students

The Panama Canal

proclaimed a republic. Then Yüan Shih-K'ai suppressed the Kuomintang and proclaimed himself Emperor. But the people of the west, though they had once supported him, abandoned him now and he committed suicide in 1916. China had still not broken completely away from her old anarchy, but the movement had begun.

The year 1914 was to be a brutal wound in the history of the world. But how did men live before the First World War ?
The townsmen were stifled in their cities. Buses and trams, either horse-drawn or electrified, offered means of transport which was often insufficient. The largest towns had just begun to build underground systems. Holidays with pay still did not exist. In France, the law on the obligatory weekly rest was only passed in 1906. It had existed in the United States since 1900. The richer classes discovered sea-bathing. The men wore long striped bathing suits, and the women, gathered pantaloons. Seaside towns became very prosperous. Vichy, a town in France famous for its health-giving waters, had seven thousand visitors in 1852, and in 1890 the number had risen to 60,000. Mountaineering was fashionable. The continental countries finally took up sports, such as lawn tennis, football, rugby, cross-country running, and became serious competition for England.

Athletics also came back into fashion. In 1896, the Frenchman Pierre de Coubertin restarted the Olympic Games at Athens, where thirteen Western nations took part. The masses also became very enthusiastic about sport. A football match in England, a boxing match in the United States, the first Tour de France in 1903 were all national events.
New enthusiasms and ideals were offered to youth by a British officer, Baden-Powell, who began the Boy Scout movement.
About 1900, electricity became increasingly popular, and was used for lighting houses and the transport systems, the trams and undergrounds. In 1901, a German electric train broke the world speed record on rail, travelling from Berlin and Zossen at a speed of 101 m.p.h. In 1895, cinemas opened in France, Germany and the United States. In 1901, Marconi sent a message across the Atlantic by wireless.
In 1883, De Dion and Bouton built a steam-powered automobile and, in 1885, Daimler and Benz built a car powered by petrol. Electric automobiles also appeared and one of these, in 1899, exceeded 100 m.p.h. In 1896, Henry Ford built his first motor car. In 1913, Louis Renault owned a factory

Assembly line in Detroit

Charles Darwin

Franz Liszt

Cubism

Expressionism

with 7,000 workers, and there were 107,000 automobiles on the French roads and 1,258,000 in America.

On 9 October, 1890, the Frenchman Clement Ader left the ground in an apparatus named the *Eole*. He rose into the air, but fell back again almost immediately. Seven years later he flew . . . for three hundred yards. After attempts by a German and several Americans, the Wright brothers finally flew up almost 300 yards into the air. At last Louis Blériot fired the world with enthusiasm when he crossed over the Pas-de-Calais in 1909 while, in 1913, Roland Garros crossed the Mediterranean from Saint Raphaël to Bizerta.

But now the clouds of war began to appear in the European sky. The direct cause was the tensions in the Balkans, where Austro-Russian rivalry was continually provoking conflicts. Russia was well aware of the fact that in supporting the Slav nationalists she risked a war. But wouldn't a war help her avoid the revolution that was menacing her?

Germany had every intention of supporting her Austrian ally; moreover, she had launched herself into the business of arming herself. Britain's cautious policy of non-committal caused Germany to think that France would not dare, in view of British neutrality, to enter into the war alongside her Russian ally.

The decisive incident occurred in June, 1914, when Archduke Franz Ferdinand, heir-apparent to the Austro-Hungarian throne, and his wife, were assassinated at Sarajevo in Bosnia. Austria saw in this outrage the opportunity of eliminating Serbia from the Balkans. She obtained support from Germany, which gave her the strength to prevent any Russian intervention.

On 23 July, Austria presented an ultimatum to Serbia. Despite Serbia's acceptance of almost all the terms of this ultimatum, Austria mobilised her armies. The whole world realised what was about to happen, and the last attempts at a compromise, during one dramatic week, were of no avail.

On 4 August the world was at war.

This war, which is generally known as the Great War, brought face to face, on the one hand, the Central European powers—Austria and Germany—to whom the Turks allied themselves and, in 1915, the Bulgarians; and, on the other hand, the Allies: the English, Russians, French, Belgians, Japanese and Italians; the Portuguese and Rumanians in 1915, and, in 1917, the Americans, Greeks and Brazilians.

The Great War developed in three distinct phases: first a war of manoeuvre,

Demonstration by the party of Young Turks

Sigmund Freud, the originator of psychoanalysis

Self portraits of two great painters: Vincent Van Gogh (ABOVE) and Paul Cézanne (BELOW).

OPPOSITE: A cinema poster from the 1913-1915 period. The brothers Auguste and Louis Jean Lumière invented the cinematograph process in 1895. They projected their film showing *Workers going home* from the Lumière workshop in Paris, in a public theatre. The film lasted one minute. But Méliès later made a true variety film and, in 1896, he built the first film studio. In 1914, studios existed in the United States and in several countries in Europe.

LEFT: A print of Paris fashion in 1912. At the beginning of the century the ladies' fashions became practical—the tailor made his appearance; footwear had rounded toes and flat heels; corsets were no longer, as they had been, instruments of torture.

The assassination at Sarajevo

The Spad, a fighting biplane

English tank

German field gun

Dadaism

in August, 1914; a static war from November, 1914 to 1917, and then another war of manoeuvre, which was to be the decisive phase of the war owing to the material aid from the Americans.

At the beginning of the war of manoeuvre, the Germans advanced up to some twenty miles from Paris, but they moved forward far too quickly and General Joffre was able to launch a counter-offensive. General Gallieni, the military governor of Paris, sent troops with great urgency, using even requisitioned Paris taxi cabs for transport.

This was the Battle of the Marne. The Germans fell back, and the two armies came to a standstill face to face. They remained crouched in trenches in a long line from Switzerland to the sea.

In the East the Russians had taken up the offensive immediately, but Hindenburg and Ludendorff crushed their army at Tannenberg and the Masurian Lakes.

During the second phase of the war, that of the static warfare, the troops lived in the trenches from 1915 to 1917 in appalling conditions.

The English fleet watched over the German coasts and blockaded all movement, and the German submarines torpedoed the Allied transport. The first military planes appeared, but they were at this stage used only for taking aerial photographs. New weapons appeared: grenades, howitzers, then asphyxiating gas. In this war of endurance, morale played a leading role. The troops lived in mud and ate only when the soup came to them.

In the year 1915, the Russians lost Poland, but Hindenburg and Ludendorff were blocked in at the Beresina River. The success of the Germans made Bulgaria decide to join the war. This proved to be catastrophic for the Serbians. On Winston Churchill's orders, two expeditions were chosen to aid the Russians and the Serbians. The first was the Dardanelles campaign, which failed. The French and English then sent troops on the second campaign to Salonika, but they arrived too late.

The Italians entered the war on 25 April on the side of the Allies, who promised them territories on their victory.

The German commander-in-chief, von Falkenhayn, decided to switch his efforts to Verdun. The offensive began on 21 February, 1916. The Germans shelled the city for twenty-four hours and then the troops attacked on an eight-mile front. A ring of defences surrounded the city, under the command of General Pétain and General Nivelle. The fortresses of Douaumont, de Vaux and de Fleury fell, in spite of heroic resistance. In the middle of

184

The October Revolution

the summer Verdun appeared to be in a dramatic position, but the French remembered Pétain's famous order: '' They shall not pass! ''

General Joffre gave the order to General Foch to commence the Battle of the Somme. This battle lasted three months. At Verdun, Nivelle succeeded in launching counter-attacks and retook the fortresses of Douaumont and de Vaux. The Germans, who had wished to exhaust the French, sustained more losses than their enemies.

The year 1917 was one of extreme weariness, when the morale of all the belligerent nations slumped. The attacks, which had been badly planned by Nivelle, notably on the Chemin des Dames, turned out to be great slaughters. After the defeats the men mutinied. Pétain restored the morale of the soldiers.

The Germans began to take their submarine warfare to bitter lengths, torpedoing unarmed cargo ships. President Wilson, upholding the right of neutral countries to unhindered navigation, decided that America must enter the war on 2 April, 1917. This was a decisive event which was to assure the victory of the Allies, especially because of the economic and financial aid provided by the United States: twenty-one billion dollars was put at the disposal of the Allies at the end of 1917. American divisions arrived during the summer of 1918 to fight beside English and French troops.

Extent of
the First World War

At the time of the American intervention, Russia had deserted. The negligence of the Russian leaders, the decimated armies and the great misery of the people brought about the revolts of March, 1917. Tsar Nicholas II abdicated. A liberal government, which constituted itself under the direction of the socialist Kerensky, attempted to continue the war. But he became more and more powerless in the eyes of the *soviets*, or councils of workers and soldiers.

Lenin and Trotsky went back to Russia in April—their return helped by Germany. On 6 and 7 November, the Bolshevik revolution triumphed, Kerensky fled to Paris and the Russian Soviet Federated Socialist Republic was proclaimed. The new leaders demanded peace with Germany. The separate peace of Brest-Litovsk was signed on 15 December, 1917.

The Germans, now rid of the opposition in the East, concentrated all their efforts on the Western front.

In France, Clemenceau became the head of the government. All the German attacks in Picardy, in Flanders, Rheims and on the Marne failed, just when they appeared to be on the point of succeeding.

The initiative now passed to the Allies. Under the direction of Foch, who

Wilson and Clemenceau

Food rationing

LEFT: **Kaiser William II, King of Prussia and Emperor of Germany from 1888 to 1918, with King Edward VII. The Kaiser's policy of military fame and colonial expansion caused fears which brought about the Triple Entente, in 1907, between England, France and Russia.**

BELOW: **The Battle of the Marne (5th–12th September, 1914). The German advance along the river was checked by French troops under the command of General Joffre, and with the help of a bold manoeuvre by General Gallieni, the military governor of Paris.**

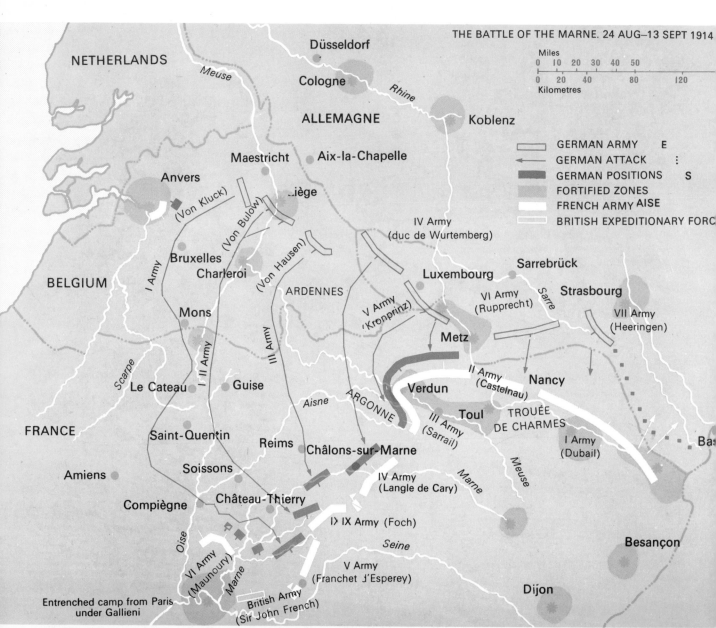

THE BATTLE OF THE MARNE. 24 AUG–13 SEPT 1914

Miles
0 10 20 30 40 50
0   20   40   80   120
Kilometres

- GERMAN ARMY
- GERMAN ATTACK
- GERMAN POSITIONS
- FORTIFIED ZONES
- FRENCH ARMY
- BRITISH EXPEDITIONARY FORC

NETHERLANDS

Düsseldorf

Meuse

Cologne

Rhine

ALLEMAGNE

Koblenz

Maestricht

Aix-la-Chapelle

Anvers

(Von Kluck)

Liège

Belgium

(Von Bulow)

IV Army
(duc de Wurtemberg)

Bruxelles

Charleroi

(Von Hausen)

ARDENNES

Luxembourg

Sarrebrück

I Army

Mons

II Army

III Army

V Army
(Kronprinz)

Metz

VI Army
(Rupprecht)

Sarre

Strasbourg

VII Army
(Heeringen)

Scarpe

Le Cateau

Guise

Aisne

ARGONNE

Verdun

II Army
(Castelnau)

Nancy

FRANCE

Saint-Quentin

Reims

Châlons-sur-Marne

III Army
(Sarrail)

Toul

TROUÉE
DE CHARMES

I Army
(Dubail)

Amiens

Soissons

IV Army
(Langle de Cary)

Marne

Meuse

Besançon

Compiègne

Château-Thierry

IX Army (Foch)

Seine

Oise

VI Army
(Maunoury)

Marne

V Army
(Franchet J'Esperey)

Dijon

Entrenched camp from Paris
under Gallieni

British Army
(Sir John French)

ABOVE: **The glorious episode of the ' taxis of the Marne '.**

BELOW: **The Renault F.T. 17 tank, nicknamed the ' Victory tank '.**

Atatürk reforms Turkey

Lenin

Trotsky

The march on Rome

Generals' Hall at Munich

had become commander of the Allied Armies, an offensive was launched along the whole front. The Germans retreated as far as the Meuse. The Bulgarians, swept over by the army of Franchet d'Esperey, asked for an armistice on 21 September, 1918. In Turkey, the English General, Allenby, was victorious, and the Turks negotiated a settlement with the English.

On the Alpine front, the Italians carried off a victory at Vittorio Veneto. The Germans now knew that they could not win the war.

On 2 November, the Austrians accepted the armistice. This was the end of the Hapsburg dynasty. Kaiser William II fled to Holland. On 9 November, the Republic was proclaimed in Berlin.

On 11 November, 1918, at 11 o'clock in the morning, the armistice was signed at Rétondes.

Casualties of the First World War totalled about ten million killed and twenty million wounded. Sixty-three out of every hundred servicemen who died came from the Allied Forces.

The Peace Conference opened in Paris in January, 1919. Thirty-two states were present, but the actual decisions were taken by the 'Big Four', comprising Wilson, Clemenceau, Lloyd George and Orlando.

On 8 January, 1918, President Wilson had brought out his 'Fourteen Points' which forcibly affirmed the right of the people to self determination, and called for the establishment of an association of nations to help to preserve world peace.

The League of Nations was established by the Treaty of Versailles, which was signed on 28 June, 1919, Germany accepting it " with the knife at its throat ".

The Treaty comprised of three types of clauses: territorial, military, and moral and financial. The territorial clauses—Alsace and Lorraine were returned to France; Schleswig went to Denmark; Posen, Upper Silesia and East Prussia, now separated from Germany by the ' corridor ' which opened access to the sea, went to Poland; Danzig, taken from Germany was declared a free city under the jurisdiction of the League of Nations; the Saar Basin, with its valuable coalfields was placed under the protection of the League of Nations for a period of fifteen years, after which its status would be decided by a plebiscite; the German colonies were entrusted to the victors under the mandate of the League of Nations.

The military clauses included the reduction of the German army to 100,000 men, and the handing over of most of her fleet to the Allies.

Charles Lindbergh

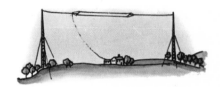

Radio antennae

The moral and financial clause: Germany had to sign a statement of guilt for the war, and begin to pay reparations of one thousand million pounds immediately, plus an annual sum, to be agreed later, for thirty years.

The Treaty of Saint Germain, signed by Austria on 11 September, 1919, and the Treaty of Trianon, by Hungary on 4th June, 1920, dismembered the Austro-Hungarian Empire. Three states benefited from these treaties: Czechoslovakia, which was a union of Slovakia and Bohemia; Serbia which, enlarged, became Yugoslavia, and Poland, which received the lower part of Silesia, a part of East German territories and the Polish Corridor.

Italy witnessed the disappearance of its hereditary enemy, the House of Hapsburg, but she considered herself wronged because President Wilson objected to her receiving the territories promised by Britain and France at the time of her entry into the war on the side of the Allies. The American Senate refused to ratify the Treaty of Versailles and the creation of the League of Nations. The United States did not want to be implicated in world politics; the people rejected the ' collective security ' of which their President had become the champion.

Joseph Stalin

Economic crises, caused by heavy government expenditure, swept through practically all of Europe, particularly Germany. The ' new rich ' were the war profiteers, industrial giants, merchants and some farmers, who provided a great contrast with the impoverished middle classes. The young people were demoralised. In many cases, where fathers had been killed in the war, mothers had become heads of families, and women were not, as yet, sufficiently adapted to this role.

In Italy, the crisis gave birth to Fascism in 1919. At the head of the movement, Benito Mussolini sought to restore the grandeur of Italy and to put an end to the disturbances which prevailed in his country.

England was faced with the Irish problem. *Sinn Fein* proclaimed the Republic of Ireland on 22 January, 1919. Lloyd George granted Ireland the status of Free State in 1922.

Briand and Stresemann

Strikes multiplied, miners and railwaymen demanded increased wages, the French government granted an eight-hour working day. Unemployment spread. In order to re-open the channels of commerce, England had to help Germany on its feet again.

In Russia, the ' White Russians ' were determined to arrest the progress of Bolshevism; they were helped by France, Britain and the Japanese. Leon Trotsky defeated the leaders of the *Whites*, Generals Denikin, Yudenich and

Marshal Pilsudski

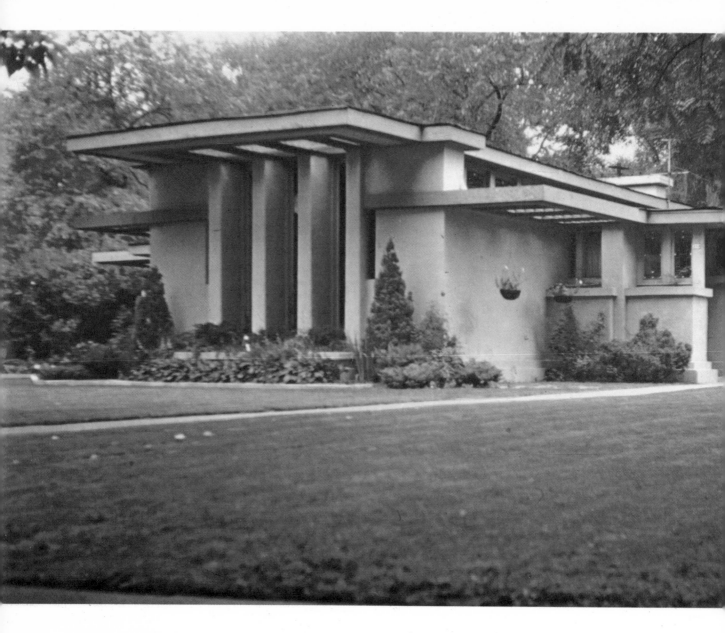

At the end of the First World War the Conference of Paris opened to prepare peace treaties. LEFT: The protagonists of the Treaty of Versailles: Wilson, Clemenceau, Balfour and Orlando.

OPPOSITE PAGE, BOTTOM: Left, the German delegates around the table where the peace treaty was signed. Right, the delegates of the signatory powers of the Treaty of Versailles.

It is necessary to include, among the architects who had a decisive influence on modern architecture, the American Frank Lloyd Wright. He maintained that the plan of a building must be conceived organically—organic architecture—and must be in harmony with the natural surroundings.

LEFT: Avery Coonley House, Illinois (1908).

RIGHT: The Manifesto of Lenin with the important points of his philosophy on the interior and exterior policy of Russia:
1. The menace from attack by the Capitalists.
2. Increase of exports.
3. Necessity of developing industry and agriculture.
4. To attempt to overcome the misery of the poor regions, with the aid of the State.

The economic crisis of 1929

Heavy Soviet industry

Sir Alexander Fleming

Teleprinter

The Japanese invading Manchuria

Kolchak, and firmly established Communist Russia. But the régime had many difficulties to face. With no fixed boundaries, Russia was faced with threats from neighbouring nations. Internally, she faced desperate problems of economic reconstruction. By 1920, industrial production had fallen to one-seventh, and agricultural production to half of pre-war levels. In two years, about seven million Russians starved to death. Lenin, realising that his harsh economic policies were not having the desired effect, rescinded them temporarily and inaugurated the New Economic Policy (N.E.P.), which returned to the principle of individual profit. Private business again began to flourish, but the government kept careful control of heavy industry. In 1921, Russia signed a trade agreement with Great Britain. In 1922, the Russian government established the Union of Soviet Socialist Republics (U.S.S.R.).

Japan benefited considerably from the World War, having acquired most of the German colonies in the Pacific, and bases in China and Siberia. Her industry was soaring. Her navy was the third largest in the world and her population was increasing apace.

China, despite great industrial progress—in 1913, China had 385,000 workers; in 1922, 3 million—was still weak and divided. The *Kuomintang*, the nationalist party, wanted to restore Chinese unity and to establish a limited socialism. In 1921, Mao Tse-tung founded the Chinese Communist Party, with no more than a hundred members. Agreement was reached between Russia and China in 1922. Colonel Chiang Kai-shek, with the help of Soviet experts, organised the new Chinese army. In 1924, Russia renounced her rights in China.

In Turkey, the sultanate was abolished and Kustapha Kemal was declared President of the Republic in 1923. Under his rule, industry and agriculture were advanced, polygamy was abolished, the position of women was raised to European status and European methods adopted generally. But the modernisation of Turkey was a lengthy process, because of the influence of Islam and the number of illiterates in the country.

In January, 1923, French and Belgian troops occupied the Ruhr valley of Germany in an attempt to force Germany to pay war compensation. The Germans there reacted with strikes and sabotage, in order to bring about a financial débâcle. German chancellor Gustav Stresemann proposed negotiations and the American Dawes Plan for the payment of reparations was adopted; this provided for the evacuation of the Ruhr.

Adolf Hitler, leading the National Socialist German Workers Party, gathered the support of kindred extremist groups to attempt the overthrow of the

Communist demonstrations in Germany

Bavarian government in the Beer Hall Putsch of 1923. The *coup* failed and Hitler was sentenced to a long term of imprisonment, along with his associates Goering and Hess. During his imprisonment he wrote *Mein Kampf* in which he set out his racial and economic theories. He was released under a general amnesty after serving only six months of his sentence.

Meanwhile, thanks to chancellor Stresemann and economist Schacht, Germany made a great recovery, aided by financial help from British and American capital, which enabled her to build up her industries.

In January, 1924, the U.S.S.R. adopted a constitution. The Council of People's Commissars was formed as the nation's formal executive and administrative organ. Lenin died on 21 January, 1924. He had saved Russia from anarchy and from fame. His name was given to Petrograd, which became Leningrad.

The war had brought prosperity to the United States. Their industries were worked to full output, and they became the premier power in the world.

The agreements of Locarno in 1925 between France, Belgium, Italy and Germany, guaranteed the frontiers of France and Belgium and brought about a general reduction of tension. In 1926, Germany entered the League of Nations, thanks to Briand.

The world conflict, in unsettling many traditional values, brought forth new talent in the cultural field. James Joyce and Somerset Maugham of Great Britain, Paul Valéry and André Gide of France, Kafka of Austria, the Americans Dos Passos and Sinclair Lewis, Thomas Mann in Germany and the Italian Pirandello, expressed in many of their works the new trends.

The Dada movement, and especially that of the *surrealists*, searched for new forms of expression: in poetry by Tristan Tzara, André Breton and Eluard, and in painting by Picabia, Ernst, Klee and Miro. The collaboration of the arts expressed itself magnificently in the *Ballet Parade* of Diaghilev, with Cocteau, Picasso and Satie. The principal musicians of the period were Stravinsky, Prokofiev, Richard Strauss, Darius Milhaud, Arthur Honneger, Bela Bartok and George Gershwin.

The whole world was seized with a great will to enjoy life and make up for lost time. These were the 'mad years'; Maurice Chevalier summed up very well the atmosphere of the era in his song, *Dans la vie faut pas s'en faire*! In the United States, this was the time of the gangsters, like Al Capone. Women became emancipated, they cut their hair, shortened their dresses, smoked cigarettes with long holders and danced the *Charleston*.

While the European countries struggled with the problems of war debts

Fashion in the 1930s

President Roosevelt

Dam on the Tennessee

First electric railway

VIEW FROM TRINITY CHURCH, LOOKING DOWN WALL STREET WITH SKETCHES OF THE BUILDINGS ON EACH SIDE.
AND THE
HEIGHTS
OF
BROOKLYN

The principal cause of the 1929 economic crisis in the United States was over-production. Warehouses were bursting with unsold goods, factories were working reduced hours and salaries were cut. The Wall Street crash, caused by the spirit of speculation which had dominated the nation in the preceding years, helped to worsen the situation. The crisis brought unemployment and hunger to fourteen million Americans and to many Europeans whose countries had economic links with the United States.

ABOVE: Wall Street, site of the American Stock Exchange since 1790.

BELOW: A hopeful queue of family men waiting to obtain public assistance.

May 29, 1932, saw the official opening in Holland of a new dike separating the North Sea from Lake Ijssel, which was overrun by sea water during the tempest of 1384. The 20-mile-long dike will allow the creation of five large polders, three of which are already complete. A polder is created by building a dike around an area of sea, lake or marsh to be drained. Then, power-driven engines pump the water from the dike-enclosed area into canals, which eventually lead to the North Sea.

BELOW: Igor Stravinsky, from a sketch by Picasso. Stravinsky, the Russian composer who became an American citizen, is an important figure in contemporary music. At the beginning of the century, his controversial ballets *The Firebird* and *Petrouchka* had a revolutionary effect on music. After 1920, he abandoned the traditional Russian themes and turned for inspiration towards neoclassicism. While still retaining his own personal style, he has been influenced, since 1952, by the Twelve Tone School. With Schönberg, he represents the major influence on contemporary music.

BELOW: Baird's television, ancestor of modern television sets. The system of tele-transmission invented by this ingenious Englishman in 1926 was adapted and improved by England and Germany between 1929 and 1936.

Scene from the Spanish Civil War; the destruction of Alkazar

Television studio

The Anti-Comintern Pact

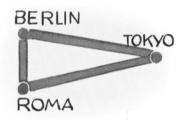

Burning of a synagogue

Research apparatus
of Otto Hahn

and reparations, the United States experienced a prosperity without precedent. Between 1923 and 1924, their production doubled. The industrialists raised salaries, and merchants began the system of credit sales. Americans began to make incredible speculations and fantastic fortunes were accumulated. One inhabitant in five owned a motor car. Telephones and radio sets, which were considered items of luxury in Europe, were available to the average American.

But this prosperity was not international. There was an agricultural crisis. Nearly half the world agricultural production was American and the Americans consumed almost all of this. This meant that 6 per cent of humanity consumed half of the world produce. Following the example of the United States, all the industrial countries shut themselves off behind customs barriers. Only money ignored the frontiers. And when, in 1929, the New York Stock Exchange collapsed, it meant bankruptcy for the whole world.

Beginning in Wall Street, New York, the financial crisis spread to Austria, Great Britain, Scandinavia, Portugal, Brazil, Egypt and Japan. Not one of these countries could escape. Only France, where speculation had remained at a more reasonable level, did not really feel the crisis until two years later. But it was particularly serious in Germany, for the Germans, now without the support of the dollar, were thrown into enormous expenses, and the repatriation of the American capital condemned 43 per cent of the population to unemployment. The working classes and the lower middle class were hardest hit. Four different armies quarrelled among themselves for power: the Communists, Republicans, ' Steel helmets ' and Nazis. At the 1930 elections, Adolf Hitler's National-Socialist Party proclaimed itself opposed to socialism, capitalism, unemployment, the Jewish race, the Treaty of Versailles, democracy. Against all of these, it carried off a victory at the legislative elections.

While France was living frugally during the economic crisis and surviving her own cabinet crises—eighteen governments between 1930 and 1936— Hitler kept his promises. The number of unemployed diminished, and he convinced the German youth that soon they would be masters of the world. '' I want to make the Germans a race of wolves ''.

On 24 July, 1934, a revolutionary attempt flared up in Vienna, and Dolfüss, the Austrian chancellor, was assassinated by Austrian Nazis. Mussolini concentrated his troops at the Brenner Pass and wrecked the *coup d'état*.

On 6 February, 1934, the Conservative leagues—of which the most important,

The Second World War

the ' Cross of Fire ' in France, was led by Colonel de La Rocque—demonstrated against the bad politicians which the Stavisky affair had just revealed in their true light. They marched on the Chamber of Deputies. There were about thirty deaths. On 9 and 13 February, the demonstrations of the Common Front for the defence of the Republic heralded the Popular Front, which was to lead the statesman Léon Blum to power.

On 13 January, 1935, ninety per cent of the Saarlanders voted for their reincorporation into Germany. In March, Hitler re-established obligatory military service. The League of Nations condemned this violation of the Versailles treaty, but this did not prevent Hitler from preparing in secret for the military reoccupation of the Rhineland. At this time the most demoniac persecution of modern times began: the persecution of the Jews. In 1935, the British and French governments endeavoured to secure a peaceful settlement with Mussolini on the basis of Ethiopian concessions, the Hoare-Laval Plan. France, Italy and Great Britain renewed the pledges taken at Locarno in 1925.

But, later in 1935, Italy invaded Ethiopia. The League of Nations condemned this act of aggression and decided to apply economic sanctions.

Winston Churchill

The League failed to prevent Italy from annexing Ethiopia and the sanctions, too, had little effect, except that they brought Mussolini much closer to Hitler.

The French did not worry much about the threat of war; the ' Maginot Line ' appeared to them invincible. Radicals, socialists and Communists formed the Popular Front.

Meanwhile, Hitler proceeded with his plans. On 7 March, at daybreak, German troops entered the Rhineland. France became more divided than ever. The English did not consider that this occupation of the Rhineland constituted a war. All that the French government could do was appeal to the League of Nations, which condemned Germany's action. But the Führer had won the first cast of the die.

English radar station

The elections carried the Popular Front to power in France. The socialist leader, Léon Blum, constituted a new government. At the end of May, strikes flared up over the whole of the country, and there were almost two million unemployed. The *Matignon Agreements* gave rise to new social reforms, of which the most popular limited the duration of weekly work to forty hours, and instituted the system of holidays with pay.

Spain, too, had a Popular Front, and Fascist groups, including the Phalanx of José Antonio Primo de Rivera. Social troubles in Spain grew worse, and in

A tank in the desert

A serious economic and financial crisis in Germany incited the skilful orator, the Führer Adolf Hitler, to form the National-Socialist Party. Having become the absolute master of his country in 1936, Hitler led a policy of aggression which was to culminate in the Second World War.

BELOW: Some Franco supporters capture an opposing group. The Phalanx in Spain, with Franco as commander-in-chief, and Fascism in Italy, under Mussolini, (BOTTOM LEFT) were the allies of German Nazism. A regime of the same nature was begun in Japan. BOTTOM RIGHT: Japanese troops during an assault on a Chinese village.

Winston Churchill is without doubt one of the greatest figures in contemporary history. In the course of his long career—he had the task of leading England twelve times—he always worked for the good of his country, guiding it with firmness, especially during the very difficult period of 1940-1941. At the head of the War Cabinet from 1940 to 1945 he took part in all the important decisions of the conflict. He was the author of several historical books, among them *The History of the Second World War*, in five volumes, and he received the 1953 Nobel prize for literature.

Rommel, nicknamed the ' Desert Fox '. After being sent to Libya in 1941 to aid the Italian troops who had been defeated by the British Army, this German general showed himself to be a daring military leader. The English succeeded, however, in snatching victory by a strong counter-offensive. In 1943, Rommel led the troops who overran the Pò valley and, in 1944, he commanded the groups of armies which took part in the Battle of Normandy.

A city ravaged by bombs

Pearl Harbour

The Normandy landing

Occupation of Berlin in 1945

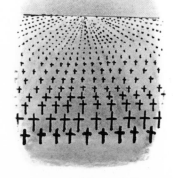

A military cemetery

Asturias and Catalonia events took on a revolutionary aspect. In July, 1936, General Franco attempted one of his *pronunciamientos*, or military *coup d'état*, to which Spain was accustomed. But Franco ran into the resistance of the government. Spain was cut in two: on one side were the Republicans, organised in an army, and on the other side the nationalists, those who supported the right, and the Fascists. But on both sides this war was full of atrocities, as well as acts of heroism and cruelty. The fall of Madrid and of Barcelona, at the beginning of 1939, marked the defeat of the Republicans. The civil war in Spain contributed to the disjointing of the Popular Front in France; for the Communists called for French intervention, the Socialists were reserved about this and the Radicals hostile. In September, 1936, the franc was devalued, and social agitation and strikes returned with renewed vigour. In 1937, Léon Blum resigned, and trouble broke out in Tunisia and Morocco.

At this time Japanese troops occupied China. This was the beginning of a war that was not to end until after Hiroshima.

The United States had still not recovered from the economic crisis of 1929. In 1933, the national revenue had halved itself. Franklin Roosevelt, who was elected President of the United States in November, 1932, gathered around him a *brains trust*, or group of men who were going to re-establish the prosperity of the country. They aimed for a planned economy with a strong social security background, known as Roosevelt's 'New Deal'.

In the U.S.S.R., after the death of Lenin two men quarrelled among themselves for power: Trotsky and Joseph Stalin, Secretary General of the Communist Party. The struggle between these two ended in the exile of Trotsky. Stalin was now master of Russia. From 1936 to 1939, the U.S.S.R. lived under a régime of terror, best illustrated in the 'purges' in the Party, and the deportation or execution of all those who opposed the Party.

Stalin was determined to reach one goal—to develop the industrial and agricultural production of the U.S.S.R., to close the gap between conditions in his country and those in the other Western nations. He compelled the peasants to cultivate the communal land in co-operatives, or *kolkhozes*, to obtain maximum use from expensive machinery. But the yield was scanty. Industry, however, made spectacular progress. Stalin's Five Year Plans set forth the objectives. Coal miner Aleksey Stakhanov, who broke all previous records in extracting coal, was held as an example to others, and bonuses for high production incited the workers to greater effort.

The U.S.S.R. became one of the great world powers.

The Spanish Civil War had again brought Italy and Germany closer together.

The new face of rebuilt Rotterdam

Hitler and Mussolini met on several occasions to confirm their agreements. On the other hand, Germany and Japan signed the Anti-Comintern Pact. Belgium declared her neutrality. In Great Britain, the leader of the Conservative Government, Neville Chamberlain, was an upholder of a peaceful policy towards the dictatorships.

The United States, still concerned with internal policies, did not consider the possibility of another war.

Finally, France's attitude in face of the rising perils was purely defensive. The forts of the Maginot Line constituted the 'essential element of the strategy'. The theoreticians took no account of the eventual importance of the aeroplane and of armoured tanks.

In the East, Poland refused to consider a military alliance which included Russia.

In this climate, Hitler could prepare his plans and envisage giving to the Reich his " vital space ".

The first act, in February—March, 1938, resulted in the *Anschluss*, that is the annexing of Austria, an event which did not arouse much reaction in the democracies of the world. But, in August, 1938, Hitler claimed the Bohemian borders of Czechoslovakia. Tension mounted in all of Europe, where troops began to be mobilised and war appeared to be imminent. Chamberlain tried by all means possible to avoid a conflict, and Mussolini offered to mediate. The conference at Munich united Hitler, Mussolini, Chamberlain and Daladier. The Western countries abandoned the borders of Bohemia, Moravia and Silesia, on Germany's promise to give up all further territorial claims. In England, clear-sighted Conservatives like Churchill and Eden protested. The moral defeat of the democracies had repercussions in the small European states and in the U.S.S.R.

On 29 August, 1939, Hitler sent an ultimatum to Warsaw. His troops entered Poland on 1 September, and, on 3 September, 1939, Great Britain and then France declared war on Germany.

In France, the armies remained face to face without fighting for several months: it was the 'phoney' war.

In April, Germany attacked Denmark and then Norway. The grand offensive had begun. On 10 May, the Germans invaded the Netherlands, Belgium, Luxembourg, crossed the Ardennes and passed over the River Meuse at Sedan. They encircled a Franco-British army at Dunkirk and stormed France. Marshal Pétain, who had replaced Paul Reynaud at the head of the government, was forced to request an armistice. On 18 June, General de Gaulle

Explosion of the atomic bomb

The flag of the United Nations

Distribution of food

The advance of the Chinese Communists

Three episodes from the Second World War.
An American parachutist about to jump from the carrier-plane in Normandy, on 6 June, 1944.

Italian soldiers in Libya.

Benito Mussolini who, following the Fascist Grand Council of 25 July, 1943, was compelled to resign. Arrested and then set free by the Germans, he prepared to board the plane that would take him to Germany.

OPPOSITE PAGE: The ruins of Nagasaki after the explosion of the atomic bomb, dropped by the Americans on 9 August, 1945.

The foundation of the State of Israel

Gandhi and Nehru

Airlift Memorial in Berlin

The N.A.T.O. flag

Mao Tse-tung

launched an appeal to the French people from London. " France has lost a battle, she has not lost the war ". However, the armistice was signed with Germany on 22 June and, on the 25 June, Italy moved in and occupied a narrow strip of territory on the French border. While the French government set itself up in an unoccupied zone at Vichy, the Wermacht occupied the northern half of France and the Atlantic coast. Five months later, Alsace was linked to Germany.

Backing Winston Churchill, the English nation resisted magnificently. The Royal Air Force won glory in the Battle of Britain and the Germans abandoned their plan of invasion.

In May, 1941, Germany appeared victorious when the German-U.S.S.R. rupture intervened. On 22 June, Hitler launched two hundred divisions, of which seventy were armoured and motorised, against the U.S.S.R. The fierce Russian resistance to the drive on Moscow and the extreme cold of winter stopped the thundering advance of the Wermacht in November.

Japan, by making a surprise attack on the American fleet at Pearl Harbour, on 7 December, 1941, extended the conflict to include the whole world. The Americans were hardly prepared for war. In several months the Japanese realised an incredible advance in South-East Asia and in the Pacific.

When the Germans reached the Caucasus, during the summer of 1942, the powers of the Axis seemed totally triumphant. But the formidable industrial machine of the United States now went into action. Resistance movements were organised in those countries which had been conquered.

This was the turning point of the war. The German Sixth Army attacked Stalingrad, an important industrial centre on the Volga, but the Russians defended the city, house by house. They launched a counter-attack which encircled 300,000 Germans and forced them to capitulate on 2 February, 1943.

The Anglo-American forces had landed in North Africa on 8 November, 1942, while the British army counter-attacked Rommel's Afrika Korps at El Alamein. On 13 May, 1943, the last German and Italian troops in North Africa surrendered in Tunisia.

At the time of the Allied disembarkation in North Africa the Germans occupied the whole of France, the French navy taking refuge in the port of Toulon so that it might not fall into German hands.

The powers of the Axis had lost the initiative. At the close of 1943, a general offensive of the Red Army liberated almost all Soviet territory. American, English and French troops landed in Sicily and then in Italy, near Naples.

Atomic power station

The Fascist Grand Council deposed and imprisoned Mussolini and the king conferred the power on Marshal Badoglio, who signed an armistice with the Allies. But the German defences were powerful and it was not until after the long and arduous battle at Monte Cassino that the Allies were able to make any advance northwards.

The year 1943 ended with the conference of Teheran, when Roosevelt, Churchill and Stalin made plans for dealing decisive blows against Germany. In captive Europe, members of the Resistance Movement were rounded up and tortured by the Nazis. Racialism reached a degree of unimaginable horror. Six million Jews were deported to concentration camps in Germany where they died, asphyxiated, in the gas chambers along with a million gypsies. Hundreds of thousands of members of the Resistance died of exhaustion in these camps. Never had a greater crime been committed by man.

Queen Elizabeth II

On 6 June, 1944, a gigantic armada landed on the Normandy beaches: the Allied Army commanded by General Eisenhower. On 15 August, another landing was staged in Provence. On 25 August, Paris was freed and General de Gaulle was acclaimed head of the free France.

By the end of the year, the Germans had evacuated nearly all French territory, excepting Vosges and Alsace, but they launched a last counter-attack in the Ardennes, which was halted by the Americans.

The people of London underwent bombardment from a new weapon: the V-1 rocket bomb.

In the east, the Red Army penetrated German territory. On 6 March, 1945, the Allies crossed the Rhine. On 25 April, American and Russian troops joined forces at Torgau, on the River Elbe. Hitler committed suicide on 30 April in Berlin, which was taken by the Russians on 2 May. Germany surrendered on 8 May.

The workers' revolt in East Berlin

The four victorious powers divided Germany into four occupation zones and, although Berlin fell within the Russian zone, the Russians agreed that it should come under the rule of all four powers.

Japan alone remained. President Truman, successor to Roosevelt who had died on 12 April, ordered the launching of a terrible new weapon against Hiroshima and, on 6 August, 1945, the first atomic bomb was exploded. Three days later another bomb ravaged Nagasaki. In compliance with the agreements made with Roosevelt at the conference of Yalta, the U.S.S.R. declared war on Japan on 8 August. Two days later Japan asked for an armistice. It was signed on 24 August. World War II was over: it had cost fifty million lives.

Kruschev

Nuclear energy, first used for cruel and murderous purposes, is today used for more peaceful ends. It constitutes the most precious and irreplaceable motive energy of the future. The nuclear reactors, or atomic piles, transform into heat the energy liberated by the controlled atomic reactions.

ABOVE: Nuclear power station at Dresden in the United States.

LEFT: Upper half of an atomic reactor. In a boiling-water reactor, water is used as a coolant.

ABOVE: **The tomb of Gandhi in New Delhi. Advocate of the liberty of India, his completely unselfish work, the elevation of moral and social principles, made him one of the noblest figures of the present epoch.**

RIGHT: **Pope John XXIII. During the short term of his pontificate he concerned himself with adapting the Church to the modern world and with re-establishing a brotherly understanding between nations.**

BELOW: **John Fitzgerald Kennedy. The young president of the United States, assassinated in Dallas, enthusiastically upheld the struggle for liberty and peace in the world.**

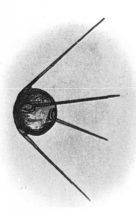

The first sputnik

The revolt in Budapest, Hungary

Atomic submarine under
the North Pole

First recovery of a
space capsule

During the war the Allies had founded the United Nations Organisation, which they hoped would be more efficacious than the former League of Nations. Its headquarters were in New York. In effect, its function was to be dominated by the rivalry between the United States and the Soviet Union. In China, the communists of Mao Tse-tung succeeded in eliminating the Kuomintang forces of Chiang Kai-shek. In January, 1949, Peking surrendered to the communist forces and, in September, the Chinese communists set up a government there.

The revival of China under a communist régime is the most notable event between 1945 and the present day. After 1950, the weight of China made itself felt in the Korean War, where the forces of the United Nations, consisting mainly of American troops, fought for three years to oppose political domination by the communists.

The Soviet Union rebuilt her devastated country. Stalin exercised a dictatorial power until his death in 1953, after which the Communist Party returned to the principle of collegiate control and found itself heading towards a certain relaxation.

In the United States, President Truman, then President Eisenhower and President Kennedy, progressed from the policy of repression to that of peaceful co-existence between socialist and capitalist nations. The two blocs did nothing to diminish their respective powers. From the moment that the Soviet Union also possessed the atomic bomb a balance of terror was born. Within these two blocs the liberty of the people was reduced. Liberty was minimised in the east, where the Hungarian revolt was pitilessly repressed by the armoured Soviets in the streets of Budapest. Liberty was limited, too, in the west, where France and England, who had intervened in Egypt to defend the Suez Canal and their dependant, the new state of Israel, against the actions of Colonel Nasser, were forced to withdraw under the joint threat of the United States and the Soviet Union.

Throughout the world, colonised nations demanded and obtained their independence. England granted it to them without struggle. India, independent in 1947, was split between the Hindus and the Moslems. The Dutch tried to conserve the Dutch Indies, but had to renounce them under pressure from the local nationalists supported by the United States. The French fought for seven years in Indo-China against the nationalists led by the communist, Ho Chi Minh. In 1954, the Geneva conference created two Vietnams: that of the North, communist, and that of the South, which soon fell under American influence.

Aid to under-developed countries

In North Africa, Tunisia and Morocco obtained their independence without too much trouble, but Algeria acquired hers only at the cost of a terrible war, which finished by putting France on the brink of civil war. A French army revolt in Algiers brought General de Gaulle back to power on 15 May, 1958—he had retired from power in 1946. It was he who, in March, 1962, authorised the Évian Agreement after the French nation had approved the agreement by a referendum on 8 April.

At the Afro-Asian Conference at Bandung in 1955, representatives from twenty-nine African and Asian nations proclaimed their anti-imperialist spirit and their refusal to commit themselves to either bloc.

Apart from political confrontations, one must note the new overtures of the Catholic Church to the problems of the time, under the guidance of Pope John XXIII and of the ecumenical council, the Second Vatican Council, which has continued its works under the pontificate of Paul VI.

Science progressed at an ever-increasing speed. Nuclear energy, terrifying weapon though it was, also carried possibilities of peaceful applications which might considerably improve the well-being of humanity. Communication satellites enabled television pictures to be broadcast simultaneously from one continent to another. Spatial research gave rise to experiments which the whole world followed excitedly.

The U.S.S.R. launched the first artificial satellite in 1957. Four years later, the Russians put the first man into space, Yuri Gagarin, who was followed by the American, John Glenn, in 1962. In December, 1965, the Americans accomplished the first space rendezvous. Two Gemini cockpits, each with two men on board, came within a yard of each other and manoeuvred in formation for five hours.

The way was being prepared for a Journey to the moon.

Firing of a rocket

**United Nations headquarters
in New York**

Greek warrior, painted on a vase.

The arch of Titus in Rome, built to commemorate the destruction of Jerusalem in 70 B.C.

CONTENTS

PREHISTORY

From the primitive cell to the first living creatures (Five thousand million years) 4
Ancestors of man 5
Homo Sapiens (60000) 5

FIRST GREAT CIVILISATIONS

Sumerians and Semites (3rd-2nd millennium BC) 8
Egyptian civilisation (3rd millennium BC) 9
Ancient Memphite Empire (2778-2263) 12
Crete under King Minos (3rd millennium BC) 13
Mesopotamia in the time of Hammurabi (1711-1669 BC) 13
New Egyptian Empire (1580-1085 BC) 16

MEDITERRANEAN WORLD

Phoenicians, nation of sailors and merchants (2nd millennium-146) 17
Hebrews before the Exodus (2nd millennium BC) 17
Ancient Greece and its heroes (1st millennium BC) 20
Athens forms a democracy (7th century BC) 24
Republic of Rome (510 BC) 24

FAR EAST

India in the time of Buddha (563-483 BC) 25
China in the time of Confucius (551-479 BC) 28

WARS OF THE ANTIQUITY

Persians attack Greece (490 BC) 28
Battle of Salamis (480 BC) 32
Greece under Pericles (463-424 BC) 36
Alexander the Great (338-323 BC) 40
Warring kingdoms in China (3rd century BC) 41
First Punic War (264-241 BC) 41

The Basilica of Saint Mary Magdalene at Vézelay

This ancient miniature depicts King Canute, monarch of England, Norway and Denmark

Francis Petrarch, poet of the Italian Renaissance

ROMAN IMPERIALISM

Greek conquests over Rome (2nd century BC) 44
Rome and Carthage (218-201 BC) 44
Julius Caesar (101-44 BC) 48
Roman peace 49
First Christians 53

BARBAROUS INVASIONS

Germans (4th century) 57
Huns of Attila (5th century) 57
Clovis, King of the Salian Franks (481-511) 60

NEW EMPIRES

Byzantium (6th century) 60
T'ang dynasty in China (7th century) 61
Mohammed and the expansion of Islam (6th century) 64
Empire of Charlemagne (742-814) 65
Normans (9th century) 69

AWAKENING OF EUROPE

First crusades (11th century) 76
Unity of France 80
Saint Louis, the crusader king (1214-1270) 80
Philip the Fair (1268-1314) 84
The Hundred Years' War, first national conflict (1337-1453) 85

THE RENAISSANCE

Golden age of Italy (15th century) 85
Great navigators: Vasco da Gama, Christopher Columbus 88
Louis XI and his vassals (1423-1483) 88
England under the first Tudors 89
Capture of Constantinople (1453) 89
The arts and letters in Europe 92
Cortés in Mexico (1519-1521) 92
Pizzaro and the conquest of Peru (1532-1541) 93
Reform (beginning of the 16th century) 96
Francis I, rival of Charles V (1494-1547) 96

Siege of a Netherlands town by the Spanish during the 17th century

A satirical illustration showing the down-trodden position of the peasants on the brink of the French Revolution

French troops enter Moscow, 1812

THE WORLD AND EUROPE 1559-1600

Wars of religion in France 100
Elizabeth I, Queen of England (1533-1603) 101
Ivan the Terrible (1530-1584) 104
The Mogul Empire 104
Splendour of the Persian realm 104
End of anarchy in Japan 108

THE GREAT CENTURY

Scientific discoveries 109
Thirty Years' War (1618-1648) 109
Cromwell's Protectorate (1649-1658) 112
England and France in the Indies 117
Jesuits in Paraguay 117
French in Canada 120
Reign of Louis XIV (1638-1715) 121
The Restoration in England (1660) 124
Peter the Great, Tsar of Russia (1672-1725) 125
War of Spanish Succession (1700-1714) 128
A new spirit 128

THE YEARS OF ENLIGHTENMENT

Frederick of Prussia (1712) and Maria Theresa of Austria (1717-1780) 129
Downfall of the French colonial empire 132
Catherine II of Russia (1729-1796) 136
War of American Independence (1755-1782) 137

THE END OF THE ANCIENT REGIME

Prelude to the Revolution 140
Flight to Varennes (1791) 144
Massacres of the French Revolution 145
Louis XVI overthrown (1793) 145
Advent of the Directory (1794) 148
Napoleonic régime (1804-1813) 149

A caricature of the German composer, Richard Wagner

Edward VII of England, with his nephew William II, Emperor of Germany

Signatories of the Treaty of Versailles: (left to right): Wilson, Clemenceau, Balfour and Orlando

19th CENTURY: RESTORATIONS AND REVOLUTIONS

Louis XVIII and the Holy Alliance (1815) 152
Latin-America liberated 153
Louis Philippe (1773-1850) 153
Industrial Revolution 156
Romanticism 160
The Second Empire and the national revolutions (1851-1870) 161
Reforms in Russia 164
War of Secession (1861-1865) 165
French expedition to Mexico (1864) 165
Awakening of Japan (1867) 168
The 1870 War 168

PRIOR TO WORLD WAR

Victorian England (1837-1901) 166
Scientific and technical discoveries 169
Colonial expansion 172
A growing power: the United States 173
Boer War (1900-1902) and Boxer Rebellion (1900) 179
End of absolutism in Russia (1905) 177
Entente Cordiale (1904) 177
Revolution in China (1911) 177
Life at the beginning of the 19th century 180
Threat of war in Europe 181

WORLD WAR I

First phase of war: the war of manoeuvre (1914) 184
Second phase of war (1915-1917) 184
The United States enter the war (2 April, 1917) 185
Bolshevik revolution (1917) 185
Foch's grand offensive (1918) 185
Allied victory (1918) 188

FAILURE OF THE PEACE

Old countries, new régimes: U.S.S.R., China, Turkey 189
The Roaring Twenties 193
Economic crisis of 1929 196
Advent of Fascist régimes 197
Civil war in Spain (1936-1939) 200
U.S.S.R.: great world power 200
Declaration of war (September, 1939) 201

A queue of unemployed during the American economic crisis of 1929

◀ Mussolini seized power in Italy in 1922

John Fitzgerald Kennedy, President of the United States, who was assassinated at Dallas in Texas

WORLD WAR II AND THE NEW ORDER

War in France (1940) 201
Pearl Harbour (7 December, 1941) 204
D-Day (6 June, 1944) 205
Capitulation of Germany and of Japan (1945) 205
East and West 208
End of colonial empires 208
Second Vatican Council 209
Experiments in space 209

SOURCE OF ILLUSTRATIONS

Page

14 (bottom right): Cairo Museum.
18 (top): Museum of Science and Technology – Milan.
22 (top): Mercurio.
23 (right): Mercurio.
30 (top left): M. Bingler.
31 (right): Hans Hinz.
34-35 (left): Metropolitan Museum of Art – New York.
34-35 (right): National Museum – Naples.
47 (bottom): Italian National Photographic Archives.
51 (top): Edinburgh University library.
51 (bottom): A. F. Kersting.
55 (bottom right): Arborio Mella.
62 (top): Municipal Library of Bayeux.
62 (bottom): Municipal Library of Bayeux.
63 (centre): Mansell Collection – London.
63 (top): Giraudon.
63 (bottom and right): John Roubier.
66-67 (top and centre): A. F. Kersting.
66-67 (bottom): British Museum.
74 (centre): Trivulziana Library – Milan.
78 (bottom right): Arborio Mella.
79 (top and left): Alinari.
79 (right): Scala.
83: Bibliothèque Nationale.
86 (top): Arborio Mella.
90 (left): Giraudon.
95: Scala.
98 (bottom): Museum of Science and Technology – Milan.

111: Arborio Mella.
114 (left): Bevilacqua.
115 (top): Scala.
115 (right): Leonard and Marjorie Gayton Photography.
118 (top): Prado Museum – Madrid.
119 (top): Rijksmuseum – Amsterdam.
122: British Museum.
124 (centre): Ashmolean Museum – Oxford.
127 (bottom): Painting by Benjamin West.
147 (top): Metropolitan Museum of Art – New York.
150 (top right): Mansell Collection – London.
159 (top): By kind permission of the Tate Gallery – London.
159 (bottom left): Prado Museum – Madrid.
165 (top): British Museum.
165 (bottom): By kind permission of Edwin Taylor.
171 (bottom): By kind permission of the Library of Congress.
174 (bottom): By kind permission of the Library of Congress.
174 (top): Marmottan Museum – Paris; Arborio Mella
　　　　Photography.
182: By kind permission of the Italian Film Library – Milan.
183: Bertarelli Library – Milan.
190 (top): Sakemoto – Photo Research Laboratory – Tokyo.
194 (top): By kind permission of the Museum of New York City.
194 (bottom): United Press.
196: Brian Keogh.
198 (centre and bottom): Keystone Press.
205 (bottom): United Press.

All other photographs have been taken from the Mondadori Archives, Milan.